CREATIVITY AND ARTISTIC DEVELOPMENT

DAVID SANDUA

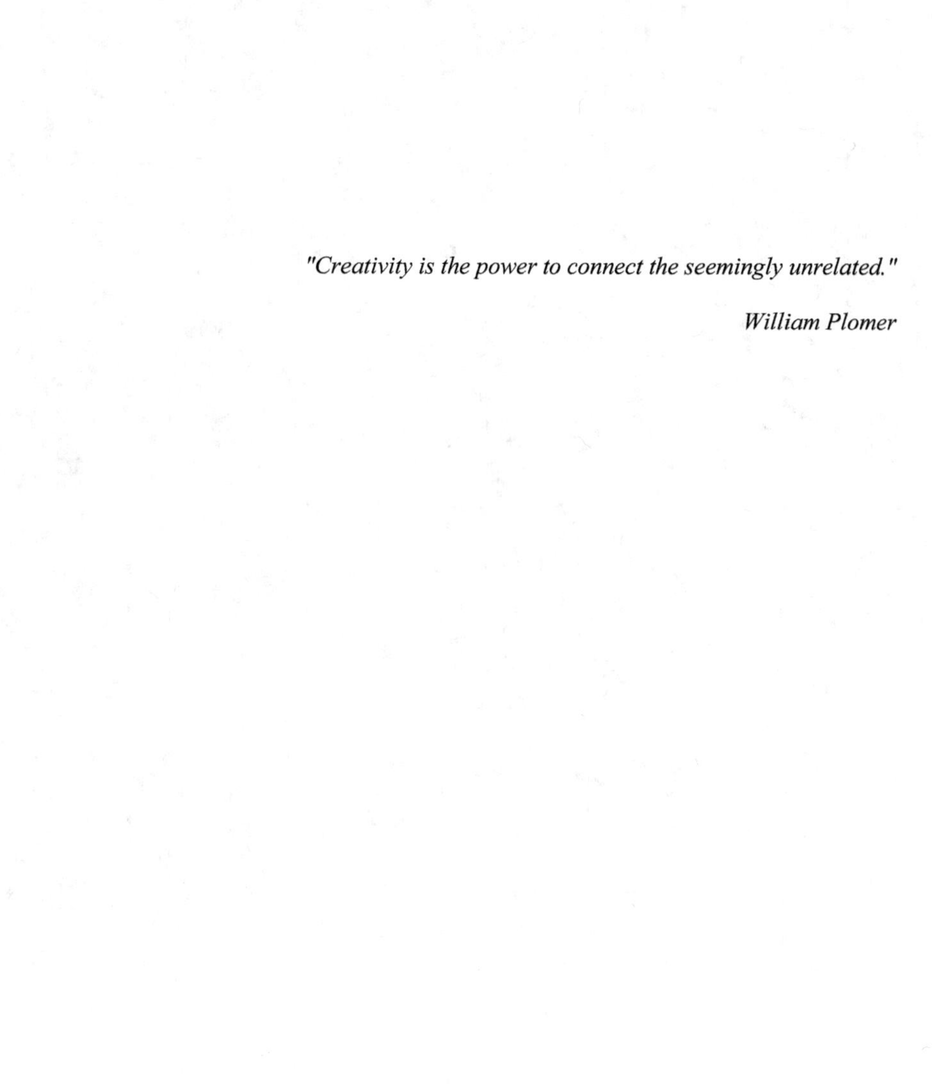

"Creativity is the power to connect the seemingly unrelated."

William Plomer

INDEX

I. INTRODUCTION

Creativity plays a pivotal part in the development of one's artistic skills, no issue what age they may be. At an early age, child often engage in various creative activities that foster their imitativeness and open up their mind to new possibility. As individuals grow older and enter into the kingdom of academe and professional life, creativity tend to be relegated to the backdrop, with more stress placed on the acquisition of knowledge and accordance to established norm. It is imperative that we recognize and promote the significance of nurturing creativity and artistic development at all stages of life. By doing so, we not only enable individuals to express themselves authentically, but we also foster a sense of invention and personal fulfillment that carries over into various aspects of life. This essay seeks to explore the grandness of encouraging creativity and the development of artistic skills throughout all ages, recognizing its valuate in personal growth, cognitive development, and overall well-being. It aims to debunk the belief that creativity is limited to certain age groups or specific domain, arguing for the want to create inclusive spaces that foster creativity for everyone. Through an exam of inquiry and example from various fields, this essay will shed illumination on the transformative power of creativity and its power to enrich individuals' life and society as a whole. By discussing the potential benefit and challenge associated with nurturing creativity in different age groups, this essay will present a comprehensive perspective of the issue and provide insight for individuals, educators, and policymakers on how to effectively support and encourage creativity in artistic development. Creativity serves as the foundation of personal growth, allowing individuals to explore their unique perspective and push the boundary of their ability. From a young age, child engage in imaginative run, unrestricted by social norm or constraint. This unrestricted run allows child to develop their creativity, enabling them to think outside the corner and experimentation with unconventional idea. As individuals progress through the educational scheme, the focusing often shifts towards accordance and the acquisition of knowledge, leaving little board for creative manifestation. Consequently, individuals may find themselves disconnected from their inner creativity, leading to a sense of fulfillment and stifled personal growth. By encouraging and fostering creativity at all ages, individuals are given the chance to reconnect with their creative selves, allowing for personal development and a sense of fulfillment in their life. Nurturing creativity and artistic skills throughout different stages of life is essential for cognitive development. Numerous study have shown that engaging in creative activities stimulates various area of the psyche, leading to improved cognitive ability such as problem-solving, critical think, and remembering keeping. Inquiry conducted by MD Aaron R. Sat at the University of Calif. riverbank, demonstrates that individuals who engage in draw and paint activities show enhanced spatial knowledge and care to particular. This cognitive benefit are not limited to specific age groups ; they extend throughout the lifetime. Promoting creativity and artistic development can contribute to cognitive function and overall mental well-being at any age. Encouraging creativity and artistic development on a broader surmount can have a positive effect on society as a whole. As individuals with various background and perspective engage in creative endeavor, they bring forth innovative idea and solution to societal challenge. This can be observed in various domains such as engineering, clientele, and the humanities. Renowned architect Zara Hadid's unconventional design have revolutionized the arena of architecture, showcasing the transformative power of creativity. By encouraging creativity and artistic development in all ages, we foster a society that is constantly evolving and adapting to the changing need and demand of the globe. Nurturing creativity and the development of artistic skills throughout all ages holds immense valuate for personal growth, cognitive development, and societal progression. By recognizing the significance of creativity and providing inclusive spaces for its refinement, individuals are empowered to express themselves authentically and tap into their full possible. Whether through engaging in artistic activities or integrating creative think into various discipline, the benefit of promoting creativity are far-reaching and impactful. It is imperative that individuals, educators, and policymakers recognize this grandness and take the necessary step to create an surrounding that encourages creativity and artistic development at all stages of life. In doing so, we can unlock the transformative power of creativity and rein its possible for personal and societal well-being.

DEFINITION OF CREATIVITY AND ARTISTIC DEVELOPMENT

Creativity is a multifaceted concept that can be defined in various way. According to psychologist Robert E. Frankel, creativity refer to the power to produce something that is both novel and valuable (Frankel, 1994) . In other phrase, creativity involves the generation of ideas or solution that are original and have some kind of practical or aesthetic deserve. Defining creativity solely in terms of trinket and valuate may be too restrictive. In the arena of psychology, some researchers argue that creativity should also be seen as a cognitive power that involves the combining, recombination, and transmutation of existing ideas (Sternberg, 2003) . This perspective of creativity emphasizes the grandness of thinking outside the corner, making connection between seemingly unrelated concepts, and engaging in divergent think. Artistic development, on the other paw, pertains specifically to the growth and refinement of artistic skills and ability. While creativity focuses on the procedure of generating new ideas, artistic development concentrate on the acquisition and hone of technical skills in a particular art form. It involves learning the fundamental principle of drawing, painting, sculpting, writing, and other form of artistic expression. As individuals progress in their artistic development, they become more proficient in their choose intermediate and gain a deeper understand of the technique, concepts, and tradition that underpin their operate. The development of creativity and artistic skills is important at all age because it enhances cognitive, emotional, social, and academic development. For child, engaging in artistic activities provides a program for self-expression, imitativeness, and exploration. Through drawing, painting, and storytelling, child can communicate their thinking, feeling, and experience in a non-verbal way. This not only helps them to develop their expressive capacity but also allows them to gain a sense of individuality and self-confidence. Art activities encourage child to think creatively, problem-solve, and think critically, which are essential skills for achiever in schooling and later in lifetime (Eisenkraft, 2003) . Artistic development is not limited to puerility ; it continues throughout adolescence and maturity. During these stage, individuals have the chance to further refine their artistic skills and explore their creative possible. Engaging in artistic activities can serve as a generator of strain succor, self-reflection, and personal growth. It allows individuals to channel their emotion, express their unique perspectives, and enlist with the surrounding globe. Artistic practice such as painting, writing, or playing a musical tool can become outlet for self-expression, mindfulness, and self-care. In plus, promoting creativity and artistic development in school and community can have broader societal benefit. Artistic activities can foster a sense of community, cultural understand, and empathy. Through collaborative project and interdisciplinary approach, individuals from different background can come together to exchange ideas, produce shared narrative, and challenge societal norm. Art teaching can help develop the next generation of innovator, entrepreneur, and problem-solvers. By nurturing creativity and artistic skills, we can cultivate individuals who can think critically, adapt to change, and find innovative solution to complex problem. Creativity and artistic development are closely intertwined concepts that contribute to cognitive, emotional, social, and academic development. Creativity involves the generation of novel and valuable ideas, while artistic development focuses on the acquisition and refinement of technical skills in a particular art form. Encouraging creativity and artistic development at all age creates opportunity for self-expression, personal growth, and community construction. It equips individuals with essential skills and mindset that are relevant in various domains of lifetime. By recognizing to valuate of creativity and artistic development, we can foster a fellowship that embraces diverse perspectives, value imitativeness and invention, and promotes human thriving.

ENCOURAGING CREATIVITY AND ARTISTIC SKILLS

One of the main reason why it is important to encourage creativity and artistic skills is because it promotes individuality and self-expression. In a society that often values accordance and adhesion to societal norm, fostering creativity allows individuals to think outside the box and express themselves in unique and meaningful way. When individuals are encouraged to explore their creative slope, they are more likely to have a feel of possession and congratulate in what they create. This can boost their self-esteem and trust, as they see to valuate of their own idea and artistic expression. Encouraging creativity and artistic skills can also lead to the development of problem-solving abilities. Engaging in creative process strengthens individuals' abilities to think critically, analyze situation, and come up with innovative solution. When confronted with obstacle or challenge, those with artistic skills are more likely to approach the problem with an open psyche and think creatively in ordering to find a resolution. This can be particularly valuable in academic and professional setting, where the ability to think creatively and outside the box is highly sought after. In plus, creativity and artistic skills also have a positive impact on mental health and well-being. Engaging in creative activities such as paint, writing, or playing a tool provides individuals with a vent for self-expression and emotional publish. This can be particularly therapeutic for those experiencing strain, anxiousness, or other mental health issue. Artistic expression allows individuals to channel their emotion and thinking into a tangible shape, aiding in the procedure of self-reflection and self-discovery. Engaging in creative activities has been shown to reduce strain level and increase feeling of felicity and fulfillment. The act of creating can be an enjoyable and immersive procedure that allows individuals to enter a commonwealth of flowing, where clock seems to fly by and all worry and stressor are momentarily forgotten. This can have a profound impact on one's overall well-being and caliber of lifetime. Creativity and artistic skills are crucial for the development of innovation and progress in society. Many of the globe's greatest invention and advancement have emerged from the creative mind of individuals who dared to think differently. Encouraging creativity and artistic skills at all age nurtures a mentality of curiosity, exploration, and experiment. It fosters a civilization where original idea are embraced and where individuals are empowered to challenge the position quo and push the boundary of what is possible. In an increasingly complex and rapidly changing globe, the ability to think creatively and adapt to new circumstance is crucial. By encouraging creativity and artistic skills, we can develop individuals who are not only capable of adapting to the challenge of the next, but also of shaping it. The grandness of encouraging creativity and artistic skills cannot be understated. It promotes individuality and self-expression, develops problem-solving abilities, enhance mental health and well-being, and drives innovation and progress in society. By fostering creativity at all age, we can create a society that values originality, curiosity, and out-of-the-box think. It is through creative expression that we can unlock the full possible of individuals and empower them to make a positive impact in the globe.

THESIS STATEMENT

Encouraging creativity and the development of artistic skills at all ages is crucial for societal progress. Artistic expression has the power to challenge existing norm and pushing boundary, leading to social change and progress. Throughout chronicle, artists have played a significant part in shaping the globe we live in today. From the Renascence to the New epoch, artists like Leonardo da Vinci, Vincent Van Gogh, and Pablo Picasso have challenged societal convention, revolutionizing the path we perceive and experience art. Art has become an intermediate through which important social and political issue are brought to illumination, leading to greater consciousness and dialog amongst individuals. Through various art forms such as paint, sculpt, lit, euphony, and movie, artists have the unique ability to communicate idea and perspective that may otherwise be over-looked or ignored. The civic redress campaign in the merge country was greatly influenced by the artistic expression of African American artists, who used their operate to shed illumination on racial unfairness and requirement equal redress. This art had a profound effect on society, sparking conversation and prompting activity. By encouraging creativity and artistic development at all ages, we provide individuals with the tool and opportunity to contribute to societal progress. Artistic expression foster empathy and understanding, essential character for a flourishing and harmonious society. Through engaging with art, individuals are exposed to different culture, perspective, and experience, promoting a greater sense of empathy and admiration for variety. Art has the power to transcend words and cultural barrier, enabling individuals to connect and relate to one another on a deeply emotional tier. Through the exploration and innovation of art, individuals develop the ability to put themselves in others' shoe, which can lead to more pity and inclusive community. Art therapy has been proven to be effective in promoting emotional well-being and enhancing empathy among individuals with mental wellness issue or injury. By encouraging creativity and artistic skills, we support the development of empathy, understanding, and pity, essential component of a prosperous and harmonious society. In plus, creative think and problem-solving skills are highly sought-after in today's complex and rapidly changing globe. Artistic development cultivates these skills, as it involves thinking outside the corner and finding innovative solution to problem. Creativity is not limited to the humanities ; it is increasingly recognized as a valuable plus in various fields, including skill, engineering, engineer, and math (stanch) . In fact, many groundbreaking scientific discovery and invention have been made by individuals who possess a creative mentality. By encouraging creativity and artistic development at all ages, we nurture the next coevals of innovator and trouble solver, equipping them with the essential skills needed to tackle the challenge of the next. Creative think foster adaptability and resiliency, allowing individuals to effectively navigate and adapt to change. In a globe that is constantly evolving, the ability to think creatively and approach problem from different angle is invaluable. Encouraging creativity and the development of artistic skills at all ages is crucial for personal increase, cognitive development, and societal progress. Artistic expression allows individuals to explore their passion, develop their unique voice, and gain a sense of fulfillment and aim. It enhances cognitive ability, promotes emotional and mental well-being, and foster self-expression and self-confidence. Art has the power to challenge societal norm, promote empathy and understanding, and contribute to social change and progress. By encouraging creativity and artistic development, we strengthen individual and collective capacity, fuel the progression of cognition and understanding, and build a more vibrant and inclusive society. Encouraging creativity and the development of artistic skills at all ages is not only beneficial for personal growth but also for the overall well-being of individuals and society as a totally. In now's fast-paced and technology-driven globe, the grandness of creativity cannot be emphasized enough. Creativity allows individuals to think outside the corner, introduce, and problem-solve effectively. It fosters a feel of imitativeness and oddity, pushing boundary and challenging convention. By developing artistic skills, individuals are able to express themselves in unique and meaningful way, conveying their thinking and emotion through various forms of art such as painting, euphony, dancing, and writing. At a young age, encouraging creativity can help children develop critical skills that will benefit them throughout their life. By engaging in creative activities such as painting, draw, and playing a musical tool, children learn to think creatively, problem-solve, and express themselves. These skills are not limited to the realm of art but are applicable in various fields such as skill, math, and entrepreneurship. A survey published in the diary of Educational Psychology found that early involvement in arts-related activities was associated with higher academic accomplishment and increased likeliness of attending college. The survey suggests that the development of artistic skills can enhance cognitive ability, improve academic execution, and foster a passion for learn. Encouraging creativity and artistic development should not be limited to puerility. In fact, it is equally important to continue nurturing these skills throughout adolescence and maturity. As individuals grow older, engaging in creative activities can provide an outlet for self-expression, reduce stress, and enhance overall well-being. The creative procedure allows individuals to disconnect from the demand of everyday lifetime and immerse themselves in an activeness that brings delight and gratification. Whether it is painting, writing, or dance, the procedure of creating something new and unique can be therapeutic and empowering, resulting in improved mental wellness and increased self-confidence. In plus to personal development, encouraging creativity and artistic development at all ages has broader societal benefit. Artistic expression allows individuals to communicate their experience, idea, and perspective with others, fostering empathy and understanding. Art has the force to evoke emotion, gainsay belief, and invigorate alter. It has been used throughout chronicle as a shape of dissent, a mean of giving vocalization to marginalized community, and a vehicle for social and political transmutation. By encouraging creativity and artistic development at all ages, we create a more inclusive and culturally diverse society that value and celebrate individual expression. Creativity and artistic development can also contribute to economic growth and innovation. In the 21st hundred, creativity and innovation are highly sought after skills in the task marketplace. According to a study conducted by Adobe, 78 % of professional believe that creativity is crucial for economic growth. The power to think creatively, solve complex problem, and adapt to new challenge

is essential in a rapidly evolving and competitive global thriftiness. By encouraging creativity and artistic development, we
cultivate a manpower that is adaptable, innovative, and capable of driving economic growth and technological advancement.
The development of artistic skills and the boost of creativity at
all ages are vital for personal growth, well-being, and societal
development. From a young age, engaging in creative activities
can help children develop critical skills that transcend beyond
the realm of art. Throughout adolescence and maturity, nurturing these skills can provide an outlet for self-expression, reduce
stress, and enhance overall well-being. The cultural and economic benefit of creativity and artistic development cannot be
overstated. By promoting creativity and artistic development,
we create a society that values individual expression, foster empathy, inspires innovation, and promotes economic growth.

II. PERSONAL GROWTH

Personal growth is a lifelong procedure that allows individuals to develop and evolve in various aspects of their lives. It encompasses physical, intellectual, emotional, and spiritual growth, as well as the development of one's creativity and artistic skills. Encouraging creativity and artistic development at all ages is crucial in fostering personal growth and can have a profound effect on individuals' lives. Engaging in creative and artistic activities provides individuals with a vent to express themselves and explore their inner thinking and emotion. This self-expression not only allows for a deeper understand of oneself but also promotes personal growth by fostering self-confidence and self-awareness. Through creative endeavors, individuals have the chance to showcase their unique perspective, idea, and talent, which can lead to a sense of fulfillment and aim. The development of artistic skills requires individuals to continuously teach and improve their craftsmanship. This procedure of learning and self-improvement cultivates a growth mindset, where individuals are willing to take risk, embracing challenge, and seek feedback to enhance their skills further. In doing so, individuals develop a sense of resiliency, tenacity, and adaptability, which are crucial qualities for personal growth in all area of life. These qualities of growth mindset are transferable to various aspects of life, including teaching, vocation, and relationship, and can contribute to overall achiever and fulfillment. In plus to personal growth, encouraging creativity and artistic development also benefits society as a totally. Artistic expression has the force to challenge societal norm, provoke critical thinking, and inspire social change. Artist have the power to create work that shed illumination on pressing social issue, raising consciousness and encouraging dialog. By fostering creativity and artistic skills, individuals are empowered to contribute to the amelioration of society through their unique perspective and creative solution. Supporting creativity and artistic development not only enhances personal growth but also enriches the cultural and social cloth of community. It is crucial to encourage creativity and the development of artistic skills at all ages. Unfortunately, societal pressure and a focusing on traditional academic subject often discourage individuals from pursuing creative endeavors. This restrictive mindset can hinder personal growth and limit the possible for invention and creativity. It is essential for educational institution, parent, and community to foster an environment that values and supports creative expression. This can be achieved through the integrating of humanities and creative activities into educational curriculum, providing admittance to artistic resource and mentorship, and celebrating and recognizing artistic achievement. It is important to recognize that creativity and artistic development are not limited to a specific age grouping. While creative ability may naturally emerge during puerility, it is never too late to cultivate and nurture these skills. In fact, engaging in creative activities later in life can have profound personal growth benefits. Older adult often experiences a sense of greening, increased self-esteem, and enhanced cognitive ability through artistic pursuit. These activities can provide a sense of aim and belong, especially during transitional period, such as retreat or empty nest syndrome. Personal growth is a lifelong journeying that encompasses various aspects of an individual's life. Encouraging creativity and the development of artistic skills at all ages is a crucial component of this procedure. The exploration of creative expression foster self-awareness, self-confidence, and personal fulfillment. The development of artistic skills cultivates a growth mindset and equips individuals with vital qualities for personal growth and achiever. Supporting creativity and artistic development benefits society as a whole by promoting critical thinking, social change, and cultural enrichment. It is imperative to create an environment that values and supports creativity, allowing individuals to thrive and reach their full possible in all stage of life.

ENHANCING SELF-EXPRESSION AND SELF-DISCOVERY

As individuals navigate their journeying through lifetime, there is a constant want for self-exploration and self-understanding. Artistic expression provides a unique boulevard for individuals to communicate their thoughts, emotions, and experiences, allowing for a deep tier of introspection. Through various art forms such as paint, writing, or dance, individuals can tap into their inmost thoughts and feeling, uncovering aspects of themselves that may have remained hidden otherwise. Artistic development offers individuals the opportunity to discover new talents and passions, fostering personal growth and fulfillment. One path in which creativity and artistic development enhance self-expression and self-discovery is by providing a safe and non-judgmental space for individuals to express their true selves. In a society that often values accordance and inhibit genuineness, many individuals may feel compelled to suppress certain aspects of their identity. Through artistic expression, individuals can break free from societal expectation and fully embrace their singularity. Paint, Allows individuals to create graphic and imaginative world without restriction, enabling them to express their deepest desire and dream. This freeing enables individuals to explore different aspect of their personality and express component of themselves that may have been suppressed or overlooked. Creativity and artistic development promote individuals to delve into the depth of their emotions, aiding in self-discovery. Artistic endeavor, such as write or euphony makeup, can provide a mean of processing complex emotions and experiences that may be difficult to articulate through other mean. To behave of creating art allows individuals to externalize their internal emotional landscape, providing them with a clear understanding of their own thoughts and feeling. Through introspection and contemplation on their artistic Creation, individuals can gain valuable insight into their own identity, helping them to navigate the complexities of their lives with enhanced self-awareness. Artistic development offers individuals the opportunity to discover new talents and passions that contribute to their overall growth and fulfillment. Engaging in various artistic practice allows individuals to explore different art forms and experimentation with different technique. In this procedure of exploration, individuals may stumble upon talents and passions that they were previously unaware of. Somebody who initially begins painting as an avocation may discover a hidden talent and develop a passion for it, which, in turn, can lead to potential vocation opportunity and a profound sense of purpose. This discovery of new talents and passions not only enhances one's self-esteem but also contributes to personal growth and development as individuals pursue avenue that bring them delight and fulfillment. Enhancing self-expression and self-discovery through creativity and artistic development is essential in enabling individuals to lead authentic, fulfilling lives. By providing a safe space for individuals to express their true selves, art allows for the exploration and festivity of individualism. Artistic endeavor can facilitate introspection, enabling individuals to gain a deeper understanding of themselves and their emotions. This self-discovery, in turn, empower individuals to navigate the complexities of their lives with enhanced self-awareness and genuineness. Artistic development offers individuals the opportunity to discover new talents and passions, contributing to personal growth and a sense of purpose. By encouraging creativity and the development of artistic skill at all age, individuals can unlock their full possible, fostering a society that value and celebrates the singularity of every individual.

ARTISTIC ACTIVITIES AS A MEANS OF SELF-EXPRESSION

Artistic activities have long been recognized as a powerful means of self-expression. Whether it is through visual arts, performing arts, or any other form of creative expression, individuals are able to communicate their thoughts, emotions, and ideas in a deeply personal and unique way. Engaging in artistic activities allows individuals to tap into their inmost thoughts and feeling, giving them a platform to express themselves authentically. One of the key benefit of artistic activities as a means of self-expression is the power to convey complex emotions and experiences that may be difficult to express through words alone. Through visual arts, individuals can create image that capture the gist of their experiences, allowing others to gain insight into their inner world. Similarly, through euphony, individuals can express their emotions and experiences through audio, evoking feeling in others that words alone cannot convey. By providing a vent for these emotions, artistic activities can help individuals to better realize and process their own experiences, as well as help others to gain a deeper understand and empathy for the artist's unique view. Artistic activities also offer individuals a sense of agency and control over their own narratives. When engaging in art, individuals have the power to shape and create their own realism, free from the constraint and limitation of the external globe. This can be particularly empowering for individuals who may feel disenfranchised or marginalized in other area of their lives. Through their art, individuals can assert their own identity, challenge societal norm, and explore alternative way of being. By providing a platform for self-expression, artistic activities can help individuals to reclaim and assert their own narratives, fostering a sense of authorization and self-actualization. Artistic activities can have a positive impact on mental health and well-being. Engaging in art has been shown to reduce strain, anxiousness, and slump, and promote a greater sense of well-being. By allowing individuals to channel their emotions into a creative vent, artistic activities can provide a healthy and constructive way to cope with and process difficult emotions. Creating art can be a form of self-care, offering individuals an infinite for self-reflection, loosening, and greening. Artistic activities can also foster a sense of community and link, providing individuals with a sense of belong and support. For those struggling with mental health issue, engaging in artistic activities can be a form of therapeutic interference, helping to improve climate, enhance self-esteem, and promote overall mental well-being. Artistic activities offer individuals a powerful means of self-expression. Through visual arts, performing arts, and other form of creative expression, individuals can communicate their thoughts, emotions, and ideas in a deeply personal and unique way. By providing a platform for self-expression, artistic activities allow individuals to convey complex emotions and experiences, promote a sense of agency and control over their own narratives, and have a positive impact on mental health and well-being. As such, it is crucial to encourage and support creativeness and the developing of artistic skill at all age, recognizing the fundamental benefit that artistic activities can have on individuals' lives.

ARTISTIC EXPLORATION LEADING TO SELF-DISCOVERY

Artistic exploration can be a transformative journey that leads to profound self-discovery. Engaging in the arts allows individuals to tap into their inner emotions, express themselves authentically, and gain a deeper understanding of their own identity. By exploring various art forms, individuals are given the chance to challenge themselves, push their boundaries, and discover hidden talents and passions. Through this process, they are able to break free from societal expectations and create a space where they can truly be themselves. Artistic exploration provides individuals with a means of self-expression that surpasses the limitation of verbal communicating. In the kingdom of art, emotions and experience can be conveyed through various medium such as paint, sculpt, or execution. This allows individuals to express their inmost thoughts and feeling in a tangible and visible form. Through creative manifestation, individuals may discover a new word that allows them to communicate emotions that would otherwise be difficult to put into phrase. This can be particularly liberating for those who struggle with expressing themselves verbally, as it provides them with a vent to communicate their thoughts and emotions more freely. In the process of artistic exploration, individuals are encouraged to shed the mask they wear in their daily life and embrace their true selves. The arts provide a fecund soil where individuals can challenge societal expectations and explore their individualism without dread of opinion. In this space, individuals are given the exemption to express their unique perspectives, belief, and value. By allowing themselves to be vulnerable and authentic, individuals may uncover aspect of their identity that they were previously unaware of. This process of self-discovery can be incredibly empowering as individuals learn to embrace and celebrate their true selves. Artistic exploration is not only about self-expression but also about pushing personal boundaries and discovering hidden talents. Engaging in various art forms allows individuals to step outside their solace zone and explore new technique, idea, and concept. This process of exploration foster personal growth and developing by challenging individuals to think differently, take risk, and experimentation with new approach. Through this exploration, individuals may discover unexpected talents and passions that they were previously unaware of. This can be a transformative feel as individuals realize their potential in area they never thought possible. Pushing personal boundaries in the arts can also lead to personal growth and a greater feel of self-confidence. The journey of artistic exploration is not limited to a specific years or phase in life. It is a lifelong process that can be pursued at any years and can continue to enrich one's life. From puerility to late maturity, art offers a means for individuals to continuously learn and discover. Whether it is through taking up a new art form or deepening one's understanding and skill in a specific intermediate, artistic exploration provides individuals with a space for growth and self-discovery. This journey allows individuals to tap into their creativeness, gain new perspectives, and develop a deeper understanding of themselves and the surrounding globe. Artistic exploration is a transformative journey that leads to profound self-discovery. By engaging in the arts, individuals can tap into their inner emotions, express themselves authentically, and gain a deeper understanding of their own identity. Artistic exploration allows individuals to challenge themselves, push their boundaries, and discover hidden talents and passions. Through this process, individuals are able to break free from societal expectations and create a space where they can truly be themselves. Whether it is through self-expression, pushing personal boundaries, or discovering hidden talents, artistic exploration provides individuals with a means of self-discovery that enriches their life at all age.

BOOSTING SELF-CONFIDENCE AND SELF-ESTEEM

Boosting self-confidence and self-esteem is another important aspect of encouraging creativity and the development of artistic skills at all age. Engaging in creative activities allows individuals to express themselves and their unique perspective. This process not only fosters a sense of personal fulfillment but also helps to build self-confidence. When individuals see their idea come to lifetime through their art, they gain a deeper appreciation for their own abilities and talents. This newfound confidence can extend beyond artistic endeavor and positively impact other areas of their life. College student who participate in art class or engage in creative project may feel more confident during presentation or public speak event. The skills and mentality gained through artistic development can empower individuals to take risks, embrace challenges, and believe in their own capability. In plus to boosting self-confidence, creative activities can also enhance self-esteem. Artistic endeavor allow individuals to explore their unique identity and express themselves authentically. Through art, individuals can discover and communicate their thinking, emotion, and experience in a way that phrase alone may not suffice. This process not only strengthens the link between the psyche and torso but also deepens the understanding and adoption of oneself. By engaging in creative activities, individuals can develop a stronger sense of self, which can lead to increased self-esteem. One way that creativity can boost self-confidence and self-esteem is through the process of pushing personal boundaries. Creativity often requires individuals to step out of their solace zone, take risks, and challenge themselves. Whether it's experimenting with new material, exploring unfamiliar technique, or tackling complex subject issue, individuals are constantly stretching the limit of their artistic abilities. By continuously pushing their personal boundaries, individuals not only develop greater artistic skills but also cultivate a sense of resiliency and confidence in their abilities to overcome obstacle. This can translate into other areas of their life, where they may be more willing to take risks, try new thing, and pursue their passion. The process of creating art also allows individuals to embrace and celebrate their imperfection. In a fellowship that often emphasizes flawlessness and accordance, engaging in creative activities encourages individuals to embrace their flaw and appreciate the stunner of imperfection. Through art, individuals learn that mistake and imperfection are not failure but rather opportunity for increase and betterment. This mentality shifting can have a profound effect on self-esteem, as individuals learn to accept and love themselves for who they are, regardless of societal expectation. Creative activities provide individuals with a sense of purpose and fulfillment. Engaging in art allows individuals to tap into their unique talents and passion, providing a sense of mean and way. When individuals are able to fully express themselves through art, they can experience a sense of fulfillment that positively impacts their overall well-being. This sense of purpose can also contribute to increased self-esteem, as individuals recognize the valuate and meaning of their creative contribution. Boosting self-confidence and self-esteem is a crucial aspect of encouraging creativity and the development of artistic skills. Creative activities provide individuals with a program to express themselves authentically and gain a deeper appreciation for their own abilities and talents. By pushing personal boundaries, embracing imperfection, and finding a sense of purpose and fulfillment, individuals can develop a stronger sense of self and cultivate higher level of self-confidence and self-esteem. This character enable individuals to navigate challenges, take risks, and pursue their creative passion with greater confidence and decision.

POSITIVE FEEDBACK AND RECOGNITION FOR ARTISTIC ACHIEVEMENTS

Despite the numerous benefit of positive feedback and recognition for artistic achievements, there are still some concern that need to be addressed. First, it is important to ensure that the recognition given is based on merit and not merely on popularity or personal connections. In an increasingly competitive globe, it is crucial for artistic development to be fostered through fair and transparent process. The recognition should be given to artists who truly deserve it, based on their endowment, attempt, and originality. This will not only encourage artists to continuously improve their skills, but also inspire others to strive for excellency. Another worry is the potential for negative effect on self-esteem and motivation when recognition becomes the sole focusing of artistic pursuit. While positive feedback and recognition are important for providing a sense of substantiation and encouragement, they should not be the sole driver of artistic development. Artists should be encouraged to create for the sake of their passion and artistic expression, rather than solely for the aim of gaining recognition or praise. This will ensure that their creativity remains authentic and unique, rather than being influenced by external expectation or trend. It is essential to acknowledge the potential bias and subjectivity in the process of giving recognition for artistic achievements. Different individual may have varying taste and preference when it comes to art, and what one person may find exceptional, another may not. It is important to recognize and celebrate the diversity of artistic expressions, and not limit recognition to a certain flair or genre. This will create a more inclusive and supportive surroundings for artists of all background and artistic vision. It is crucial to provide opportunities for constructive criticism and feedback alongside positive recognition. While positive feedback is essential for boosting self-confidence and motivation, constructive criticism can play a vital part in artistic increase. By identifying area for betterment and offer direction, artists can further develop their skills and refine their artistic flair. The combining of positive recognition and constructive criticism creates a balanced overture that encourages both self-expression and artistic development. Positive feedback and recognition for artistic achievements have many advantages in promoting creativity and artistic development. They provide substantiation, encouragement, and motivation for artists, helping them to overcome challenge and continue pursuing their passion. Recognition also fosters a sense of congratulate and achievement, which can contribute to increased self-esteem and trust. It is important to ensure that recognition is based on merit, rather than popularity or personal connections, to maintain candor and transparency. Artists should be encouraged to create for the sake of their passion and artistic expression, rather than solely for recognition or praise. The potential bias and subjectivity in the process of recognizing artistic achievements should also be acknowledged, and effort should be made to celebrate the diversity of artistic expressions. Opportunities for constructive criticism and feedback should be provided alongside positive recognition to support artists' continued increase and development. By striking an equilibrium between positive recognition and constructive criticism, we can create an surrounding that encourages creativity and the development of artistic skills at all ages.

OVERCOMING CHALLENGES AND BUILDING RESILIENCE THROUGH ARTISTIC ENDEAVORS

Artistic endeavors have the force to help individuals overcome challenges and build resilience. Engaging in creative activities such as painting, writing, or playing a tool can provide an outlet for self-expression and service as a shape of therapy. By channeling their emotion and experience into their art, individuals are able to process and make sense of difficult situation in their life. Those struggling with mental wellness issue can find comfort in painting or writing to express their feeling in a non-verbal path. Artistic endeavors can also provide a sense of achievement and boost self-esteem, as individuals see their work come to life and receive positive feedback from others. This can be particularly empowering for individuals who have faced setback or hardship. By seeing the tangible outcome of their effort, they gain a renewed sense of confidence and notion in their ability. The procedure of creating art also requires tenacity and problem-solving skill. Artist often encounter obstacle and challenges along the path, such as a painting not turning out as they had envisioned or facing an author's blocking. The act of persisting through these challenges and finding creative solution to overcome them build resilience and adaptability. This character are transferable to other area of life, enabling individuals to face future challenges with a greater sense of confidence and creativity. Artistic endeavors can also foster a sense of belong and community. In grouping setting such as art class or writing workshop, individuals can connect with like-minded individuals who deal similar passion and interest. This sense of community provides a supporting scheme that can help individuals navigate through challenges and setback. By sharing their work and receiving feedback from others, individuals can gain new perspectives and insight, which can further fuel their artistic development. Engaging in artistic endeavors can also cultivate empathy and understanding. Creating art often involves delving into different perspectives and exploring diverse narrative. By exploring different theme and subject in their creative work, individuals can develop a deeper understanding of the human feel and the challenges faced by others. This can lead to increased empathy and pity towards others, promoting a more inclusive and understanding fellowship. Engaging in artistic endeavors can also have a positive effect on overall well-being. Numerous study have shown that participating in creative activities can reduce strain, boost climate, and improve overall psychological wellness. The act of creating can be deeply therapeutic, helping individuals to relax, focus on the present minute, and find delight in the procedure. Whether it is losing oneself in the beat of playing a tool or immersing oneself in the color and texture of painting, artistic endeavors provide individuals with a much-needed elude from the demand and pressure of daily life. Artistic endeavors have the possible to help individuals overcome challenges and build resilience. By providing an outlet for self-expression, boosting self-esteem, and fostering a sense of community, artistic activities can empower individuals to face hardship with creativity and potency. Engaging in artistic endeavors can cultivate empathy, promote personal growth, and improve overall well-being. At all age and stage of life, creativity and artistic development should be encouraged and embraced as essential tool for personal growth and resilience. Encouraging creativity and the development of artistic skills at all ages has several benefits that can positively impact individuals and society as a whole. First and foremost, engaging in creative activity allows individuals to express themselves and their unique view on the world. Artistic endeavors provide a vent for emotion, thinking, and experience that may otherwise remain unexpressed or repressed. This process of self-expression can be incredibly cathartic, leading to improved mental well-being and reduced strain level. Creativity foster self-discovery and personal increase by promoting introspection and contemplation. Through artistic expression, individuals can gain a deeper understand of themselves and their spot within the world, leading to increased self-confidence and self-awareness. The development of artistic skills nurtures critical thinking and problem-solving abilities. Engaging in creative activity requires individuals to think outside the corner, explore alternative solution, and take risk. This process stimulates the psyche and enhances cognitive function, leading to improved problem-solving skills that can be applied in various area of life. Creativity encourage individuals to question established norm and gainsay societal convention, fostering a culture of invention and progression. Artist have the unique power to disrupt the position quo and introduce new idea and perspective, leading to societal paradigm shift and advancement in various fields. Encouraging creativity has societal benefit as well. The humanities have the force to unite community and foster social cohesion. Artistic endeavors bring masses together, encouraging collaboration, empathy, and understand. Whether it be through attending a dramaturgy execution, visiting a museum, or participating in a community arts design, individuals are given the opportunity to connect with others and deal in the collective human feel. This feel of community and shared mean promote social resiliency and can strengthen the bond between individuals from various background. The humanities lend to the thriftiness by generating job and boosting local business. A flourishing humanities' scenery attracts tourist, stimulates tourism receipts, and enhances the overall caliber of life for resident. Fostering creativity and artistic development at all ages is essential for the conservation of culture and inheritance. Art serves as a clock encapsulate, capturing the gist of a particular clock point and reflecting the value, belief, and experience of a community or society. By encouraging artistic expression, we ensure that our culture and chronicle are preserved and celebrated for future generation. Art provides a program for marginalized voice to be heard and represented, allowing for a more inclusive and diverse society. Creativity plays a crucial part in teaching and academic accomplishment. The traditional teaching scheme often prioritizes linear thinking and accordance, neglecting the grandness of creative thinking. Inquiry has shown that incorporating creativity into the syllabus enhances student' participation, motivating, and overall execution. Creative activity promote hands-on learn, critical thinking, and problem-solving skills. Art teaching has been linked to improved cognitive abilities, such as enhanced remembering, care bridge, and spatial news. By nurturing creativity and artistic skills in student, we can create a more dynamic and holistic learn surroundings that fosters a passion for learning and encourages student to reach their full possible. Encouraging creativity and the development of artistic skills at all ages is not only personally fulfilling but also beneficial for society as a whole. By providing individuals with the opportunity to express themselves, fostering critical thinking and problem-solving abilities, promoting social cohesion, preserving culture and inheritance, and enhancing teaching, we can harness the transformative force of creativity to create a more vibrant, inclusive, and resilient society. It is imperative that we recognize and prioritize to valuate of creativity in all its form and ensure that it is actively cultivated and supported in our community.

III. COGNITIVE DEVELOPMENT

Cognitive development refers to the growth and transmutation of an individual's mental abilities and process throughout their lifetime. This includes the development of perception, attention, memory, language, problem-solving, and reasoning skills. Creativity and artistic development play a crucial part in enhancing cognitive development in individuals of all ages. Research has shown that engaging in creative activities and developing artistic skills can lead to improvement in cognitive abilities. When individuals engage in artistic activities, such as painting, drawing, or playing a musical instrument, they are required to use their perceptual and centrifugal skills to create something visually appealing or produce a melodious audio. This process of creating art stimulates the psyche and helps in developing and refining these skills. Individuals need to pay attention to detail, make decision, and solve problem while engaging in artistic endeavors. This cognitive process not only contribute to the development of artistic skills but also enhance overall cognitive abilities. Artistic development promotes the growth of memory and language skills. When individuals engage in activities such as storytelling, writing, or memorizing script for theatrical performance, they are actively exercising their memory and language abilities. Creating and remembering narrative or lines, understanding the construction and syntax of sentence, and using appropriate vocabulary all require cognitive attempt. By consistently engaging in artistic activities, individuals can strengthen their memory and language skills, which are vital component of cognitive development. Artistic development foster critical and creative thinking. When individuals engage in artistic endeavors, they are often required to think critically about various aspects. Painter need to think critically about the positioning of color and lines, musician need to think about the harmonization of different note, and actor need to think about portraying emotion authentically. This process of critical thinking helps to enhance problem-solving and reasoning skills. Artistic development encourages individuals to think creatively, to explore new idea, and to challenge conventional thinking. By encouraging creativity and artistic development, individuals are not only expanding their cognitive abilities but are also developing the skills necessary to think critically and creatively in other area of their life. It is important to note that cognitive development is not limited to specific age group. While it is true that cognitive abilities develop rapidly during childhood and adolescence, cognitive growth continues throughout maturity and even in old age. It is crucial to encourage creativity and artistic development at all ages to maximize cognitive possible. Research has shown that engaging in artistic activities and nurturing creativity can have positive effect on cognitive operate in older individuals. Study have demonstrated that involvement in activities such as painting, dancing, or playing a musical instrument can improve attention, memory, and problem-solving skills in older adult. These finding suggest that the benefit of artistic development on cognitive operate extend well beyond childhood and adolescence. Cognitive development is a lifelong process that can be enhanced through creativity and artistic development. Engaging in artistic activities and developing artistic skills not only stimulates the psyche but also promotes the growth and betterment of perception, attention, memory, language, problem-solving, and reasoning abilities. Artistic development encourages critical and creative thinking, which are valuable skills in various domains of lifetime. It is crucial to encourage creativity and the development of artistic skills at all ages, as this can significantly contribute to an individual's cognitive development and overall well-being.

ENHANCING CRITICAL THINKING AND PROBLEM-SOLVING SKILLS

Critical thinking involves analyzing info, evaluating argument, and making informed decision. It is a skill that is highly valued in the work and can lead to increased achiever in one's vocation. Critical thinking is essential for navigating and understanding the complex and diverse globe we live in. By encouraging creativity and the development of artistic skills, individuals are able to strengthen their critical thinking ability. Artistic activities, such as painting, writing, and playing a tool, require individuals to think critically and problem-solve. When painting a photograph, an individual must analyze how color and shape interact with one another, evaluate the makeup and equilibrium of the art, and make decision about how to best represent their subject issue. These skills transfer over into other areas of lifetime, helping individuals to approach problems with a more analytical and strategic mindset. Artistic development can also foster problem-solving skills. When engaging in creative activities, individuals are often faced with challenge that require them to think outside the corner and find innovative solutions. When writing a tale, an individual may encounter a diagram maw that needs to be resolved. This forces them to brainstorm different ideas, evaluate the consequence of each alternative, and ultimately choose the most effective solution. The process of artistic development encourages individuals to approach problems with an open mind and consider multiple perspectives. This can lead to increased tractability in thinking and the power to adapt to new and unexpected situation. Artistic development can enhance critical thinking and problem-solving skills by promoting a sense of curiosity and inquiry. Engaging in creative activities encourages individuals to explore different ideas, ask question, and seek answer. This mindset of curiosity and inquiry is fundamental to critical thinking, as it encourages individuals to question established norm and seek out new and innovative solutions. By nurturing this sense of curiosity through artistic development, individuals are more likely to approach problems with a willingness to learn and explore different perspectives. This can lead to more creative and effective problem-solving strategy. Engaging in creative activities provides individuals with a platform to express their thoughts and ideas in a unique and personal way. Artistic development allows individuals to communicate through various medium, such as painting, writing, or euphony, which can be a powerful form of self-expression. By expressing themselves creatively, individuals are able to explore and articulate their thoughts, emotion, and experience. This process of self-expression can enhance critical thinking skills by encouraging individuals to reflect on their own perspectives and consider different viewpoint. Through artistic development, individuals can develop a greater sense of self-awareness and empathy, which are crucial component of critical thinking and problem-solving. Enhancing critical thinking and problem-solving skills is essential for personal and professional increase. By encouraging creativity and the development of artistic skills, individuals can strengthen these skills in a unique and meaningful path. Artistic activities require individuals to think critically and problem-solve, fostering a strategic mindset that can be applied to various areas of lifetime. Creative endeavor foster curiosity and inquiry, promoting a willingness to explore different perspectives and seek innovative solutions. Engaging in creative activities provides individuals with a platform for self-expression, enhancing self-awareness and empathy. Promoting creativity and artistic development at all ages is crucial for enhancing critical thinking and problem-solving skills.

ARTISTIC ACTIVITIES REQUIRING ANALYSIS AND DECISION-MAKING

In plus to promoting self-expression, artistic activities requiring analysis and decision-making can also enhance critical think skills. The process of creating art often involves assessing different option and making informed decision about the composition, coloration palette, and overall designing. A cat amount may need to analyze various brushing stroke and technique to achieve the desired consequence, while a lens man might evaluate different angle and lighting weather to capture the perfect shooting. Through these experience, individuals can develop their analytical skills and learn to think critically about their artistic choice. By asking themselves question such as "Which color should I use to convey the desired climate ?" Or "What composition will best convey my content ?". Artist become more adept at making thoughtful decision and evaluating the potential outcome of each selection. This ability to analyze, evaluate, and make decision extends not only to the artistic kingdom but also to other area of life. Artistic activities requiring analysis and decision-making also nurture problem-solving skills. When faced with challenge or obstacle during the creative process, artist must find innovative way to overcome them. A carver may encounter difficulty while shaping a slice of mud, but by experimenting with different technique and approach, they can find a resolution to the trouble. This process of tribulation and mistake foster a problem-solving mentality that can transfer to other domain of life. By cultivating creativity and encouraging artistic development, individuals become better equipped to tackle complex problem with a flexible and resourceful overture. Engaging in artistic activities that demand analysis and decision-making can also foster emotional intelligence. Artist often seeks to convey specific emotions or message through their operate, which requires them to tap into their own emotions and empathize with those of others. When creating a figurative sculpt, an artist must consider the topic's stance, facial manifestation, and torso words to accurately represent a particular emotion. In the process, artists develop a deeper understanding of human emotions and enhance their ability to empathize with others. This increased emotional intelligence can have far-reaching benefit, as it allows individuals to connect with others on a deeper tier, understand different perspective, and respond compassionately to various situations. Artistic activities requiring analysis and decision-making also contribute to the development of aesthetic appreciation. By engaging in the innovation of art and critically analyzing different artistic style, individuals expand their understanding and appreciation for various forms of artistic manifestation. As they explore different artistic technique, medium, and concept, they develop a discern eyeball for caliber, composition, and creativity. This heightened aesthetic sensitiveness can enhance one's delectation and understanding of art, enabling them to recognize and valuate the intricacy of artistic work. Artistic activities requiring analysis and decision-making not only promote self-expression but also enhance critical think, problem-solving, emotional intelligence, and aesthetic appreciation. By undertaking artistic endeavor that demand analytical think and decision-making, individuals develop their ability to assess choice, solve problem, empathize with others, and appreciate

the stunner in an assortment of artistic expression. As we encourage and foster creativity and artistic development at all
age, we empower individuals to engage in activities that enrich
their cognitive, emotional, and aesthetic capacity, ultimately
contributing to their overall personal and intellectual increase.

ARTISTIC PROBLEM-SOLVING AS A TRANSFERABLE SKILL

Artistic problem-solving is a crucial transferable skill that can significantly benefit individuals in various aspects of their lives. In today's rapidly changing globe, creative thinking and problem-solving ability are highly sought after by employer across different industry. It is not just in the professional kingdom that artistic problem-solving is valuable ; it also plays a critical role in personal growth and development. One of the primary benefit of artistic problem-solving is its ability to foster critical thinking. In the process of creating art, individuals are constantly faced with different challenge and obstacle that require them to think creatively and find innovative solutions. Whether it is choosing the right color for a paint, composing a tune, or choreographing a dancing mundane, artists are constantly engaging in problem-solving activity. This not only enhances their ability to think critically but also allows them to approach problem from different perspective, leading to more well-rounded solutions. Artistic problem-solving promote originality and the ability to think outside the corner. Artists are often confronted with limitation, such as a limited budget or deficiency of resource, which require them to think creatively in ordering to overcome this obstacle. This encourages individuals to explore unconventional approach and push the boundary of their creativeness. By constantly seeking new and innovative solutions, artists develop a deep feel of originality and an open-mindedness that can be applied to various domains of their lives. Artistic problem-solving also has a significant effect on emotional intelligence. Through the process of creating art, individuals are able to express and explore their emotion in a safe and non-judgmental surroundings. This helps individuals develop a better understand of their own emotion as well as the emotion of others. Artists are often required to convey specific emotion through their operate, requiring them to tap into their own emotional intelligence. This enables them to communicate effectively with others and develop stronger interpersonal relationship. The ability to understand and interpret emotion is crucial in problem-solving, as it allows individuals to empathize with others and gain a deeper perceptiveness into their need and desire. Artistic problem-solving cultivate resilience and tenacity. Artistic endeavor are rarely smooth sail ; artists often face setbacks, criticism, and failure along the path. Through these challenge, individuals learn to accept and embrace loser as component of the creative process. They develop resilience and the ability to bounce back from setbacks, which is an essential skill in all area of lifetime. Artists also learn to persevere and remain committed to their goal, even in to confront of hardship. This decision and perseverance are transferable skill that can greatly benefit individuals in their personal and professional pursuit. Artistic problem-solving is an invaluable transferable skill that has wide-ranging benefit. From fostering critical thinking and originality to enhancing emotional intelligence and resilience, artistic problem-solving plays a pivotal role in personal growth and development. Whether individuals pursue a vocation in the humanities or not, the ability to think creatively and find innovative solutions is highly sought after in today's globe. As such, it is imperative that individuals are encouraged to develop their artistic skill and harness the force of artistic problem-solving at all age.

STIMULATING IMAGINATION AND CREATIVITY

Stimulating imagination and creativity has immense benefit in various aspects of lifetime, including education, problem-solving, and personal growth. In an educational set, fostering imagination and creativity allows student to think critically and outside the corner. It encourages them to explore different perspective and idea, enabling them to gain a deeper understand of the subject issue. When student are assigned a creative design like writing a tale or designing an experimentation, they are not confined to a put of rule or predetermined outcome. Instead, they have the exemption to use their imagination and experimentation with different possibility, leading to innovative and unique solutions. This overture not only enhances their learning feel but also cultivates their creativity and problem-solving skills. Creativity plays a vital role in problem-solving. In our rapidly changing world, the power to think creatively and find innovative solutions is highly valued. When faced with a complex problem, individuals who can think outside the corner are more likely to come up with unconventional and effective solutions. Creative individuals can see connection and pattern that others might overlook, allowing them to identify novel approach to solve problem. They are more willing to take risk and embracing failure, understanding that setback provides valuable learn opportunity. By encouraging imagination and creativity, we are equipping individuals with the necessary skills to tackle complex challenge and adjust to an ever-evolving world. Stimulating imagination and creativity has a profound effect on personal growth. Engaging in creative activities allows individuals to express themselves and explore their thinking and emotion. Through various forms of artwork, such as paint, writing, or dance, individuals can communicate their experience, belief, and aspiration, fostering introspection and self-discovery. This procedure not only enhances one's self-awareness but also promotes emotional well-being and resiliency. Engaging in creative endeavor provides individuals with a feel of aim and fulfillment, contributing to their overall felicity and lifetime gratification. Stimulating imagination and creativity is crucial for the developing of artistic skills and fostering personal growth. It encourages individuals to think critically, explore different perspective, and come up with innovative solutions. By promoting imagination and creativity in education, we are equipping student with essential skills to navigate an increasingly complex world. Creativity plays a significant role in problem-solving, allowing individuals to find unconventional and effective solutions. Engaging in creative activities promotes self-expression, introspection, and emotional well-being. It is important to create an surrounding that recognizes and nurtures creativity at all ages, supporting individuals in their artistic developing and personal growth.

ARTISTIC ACTIVITIES FOSTERING IMAGINATIVE THINKING

One of the main benefit of artistic activities is that they foster imaginative thinking. Through engagement in the arts, individuals are encouraged to think outside the box, explore new possibility, and challenge conventional ways of thinking. Artistic activities provide a chance for individuals to unleash their imitativeness and tap into their creative possible. When painting a photograph, an artist has the exemption to create their own unique interpreting of the subject issue. They can choose to use different color, texture, and technique to convey their thoughts and emotion. This process of imaginative thinking allows individuals to express themselves in a way that is not limited by the constraint of realism. Artistic activities often require problem-solving skill, as artists are constantly faced with challenge and obstacle that they must overcome to bring their idea to realization. This want for problem-solving encourages individuals to think creatively and find innovative solution to artistic problem. By approaching these challenge with an open psyche and a willingness to experiment, artists are able to expand their imaginative thinking abilities and develop new ways of approaching their work. Artistic activities provide individuals with a platform for self-expression and self-discovery. Through the innovation of art, individuals are able to explore their own thoughts, feelings, and experiences in a meaningful and personal way. This process of self-reflection not only fosters self-awareness but also allows individuals to gain a deeper understand of themselves and the world around them. When writing a poem, a poet may reflect on their own emotion and experiences, using imaging and metaphor to convey their inmost thoughts and feelings. This act of self-expression can be incredibly cathartic and can provide individuals with a feel of publish and heal. Artistic activities can also encourage individuals to think critically and analyze the world around them. Through engagement with different forms of art, individuals are exposed to different perspectives and idea, stimulating their critical thinking skill. When analyzing a piece of lit, individuals are encouraged to think critically about the theme, motif, and symbolization that the writer has employed. This critical psychoanalysis requires individuals to consider multiple perspectives and interpretation, fostering a deeper understand and admiration for the arts. Artistic activities can also foster interdisciplinary thinking as individuals explore the connections between different art forms and discipline. A Terpsichore may draw aspiration from a piece of euphony or a visual artist may incorporate element of storytelling into their art. This interdisciplinary overture encourages individuals to think beyond the boundary of a single art form and make connections between different area of survey. By doing so, individuals are able to expand their creative thinking abilities and approach their work from a more holistic and integrated perspective. Artistic activities play a vital part in fostering imaginative thinking. They provide individuals with a platform to express themselves, explore their own thoughts and feelings, and challenge conventional ways of thinking. Through engagement with the arts, individuals are encouraged to think outside the box, problem-solve, and analyze the world around them. Artistic activities promote interdisciplinary thinking and encourage individuals to make connections between different discipline and art forms. It is essential that individuals of all ages are encouraged to engage in artistic activities, as they have the potential to enhance creative thinking and personal developing.

CREATIVE THINKING AS A CATALYST FOR INNOVATION AND PROGRESS

At the individual level, creative thinking allows individuals to see thing from different perspectives, challenge existing norms, and generate new ideas and solutions. It encourages individuals to think outside the box and explore unconventional approach to problem-solving. The power to think creatively is particularly valuable in today's fast-paced and complex world, where traditional solutions may no longer be effective. In ordering to foster creative thinking, individuals must be encouraged to embrace incertitude and take risk, as these are often the rearing soil for breakthrough ideas. Individuals should be provided with opportunity to engage in activity that stimulate their imitativeness and encourage them to explore new possibilities. This could include vulnerability to various art forms, such as visual arts, euphony, dancing, and lit, which can not only inspire creativeness but also enhance cognitive ability and emotional news. The development of creative thinking skills can be cultivated through educational practice that promote critical thinking, problem-solving, and divergent thinking. These practice involve encouraging multiple perspectives, generating alternative solutions, and questioning assumption. By equipping individuals with the tool to think creatively, they are empowered to contribute to societal progress and make a meaningful affect. On a collective level, creative thinking is essential for promoting innovation and driving progress in various fields. Creativeness fuels breakthroughs in technology, science, business, and the arts, leading to advancements that shape society. Innovative technology such as smartphones, electric vehicle, and social medium platform have revolutionized the way we live, operate, and interact with each other. These breakthroughs would not have been possible without the creative mind who challenged existing norms and imagined new possibilities. Creative thinking is instrumental in addressing complex societal challenges, such as clime alter, impoverishment, and healthcare. By thinking creatively, individuals and organizations can develop innovative solutions that may not have previously been considered. The designing of sustainable building, the development of renewable vitality source, and the execution of inclusive healthcare system all require creative thinking to bring about positive alter. In plus, creative thinking plays a crucial role in promoting economic growth and fight. In today's globalized and rapidly evolving economy, organizations must constantly innovate and adapt to stay ahead. Creative thinking enables organizations to identify new marketplace opportunity, develop unique product and service, and find innovative way to meet client need. Company that embrace creative thinking as part of their civilization are more likely to attract top endowment, foster collaboration and variety, and generate a competitive vantage. Creative thinking can lead to the innovation of new industry and the transmutation of existing one. It has the force to disrupt traditional business model and drive economic transmutation. The rising of the sharing economy, e-commerce, and the gig economy are all product of creative thinking that has reshaped the way we do business. Creative thinking serves as a catalyst for innovation and progress at both the individual and collective levels. It enables individuals to think outside the box, challenge existing norms, and generate new ideas and solutions. Creative thinking is particularly valuable in today's complex and fast-paced world, where traditional solutions may no longer do. On a collective level, creative thinking is crucial for promoting innovation, driving progress, and addressing complex societal challenges. It fuels breakthroughs in various fields, including technology, science, business, and the arts, leading to advancements that shape society. Creative thinking plays a vital role in promoting economic growth and fight, as it enables organizations to innovate and adapt to stay ahead. It is essential to encourage and cultivate creative thinking skills at all age to nurture innovation, progress, and societal development. Encouraging creativity and the development of artistic skills at all ages not only benefits individuals but also society as a whole. Creativity and artistic manifestation have the force to provoke think, gainsay norm, and stimulate dialog. By fostering an environment that values and supports creativity, we allow for the exploration and dissemination of unique perspectives, ultimately promoting variety and inclusivity. This is particularly important in now's interconnected and diverse globe, where the interchange of idea and perspectives is crucial for societal progression and understanding. The refinement of creativity and artistic skills can also provide numerous personal and psychological benefits. Engaging in creative activities has been shown to reduce strain, improve climate, and enhance overall well-being. The act of creating art allows individuals to express their emotion, experience, and thinking in a tangible shape, providing a feel of duration and self-reflection. This procedure of self-expression can be particularly beneficial for individuals dealing with injury or mental wellness issue, as it can serve as a therapeutic vent for process and heal. Creativity and artistic development have been linked to cognitive and intellectual growth. Participating in artistic activities, such as draw, paint, or playing a musical tool, can enhance critical thinking, problem-solving, and decision-making skills. These activities require individuals to think outside the corner, experimentation with different technique, and make choice based on their artistic hunch. Such cognitive process can transfer into other area of life, improving creative problem-solving ability and fostering a flexible and adaptable mentality. Encouraging creativity and the development of artistic skills at all ages can lead to the uncovering and nurture of endowment. By providing opportunity for individuals to explore different art form, we unlock their potential and allow them to uncover hidden talent. This is particularly important in early puerility, as it is during this point that many individuals discover their love for a specific artistic correction. By fostering a supportive and encouraging environment, we can empower young artist to pursue their passion and develop their artistic skills, potentially leading to future careers or lifelong hobbies. Creativity and artistic development can also contribute to economic growth and innovation. The creative industry, including visual arts, performing arts, designing, and medium, are a significant driver of economic activeness. The promotion and support of creative individuals and industry can lead to job creation, increase tourism, and stimulate innovation and entrepreneurship. By encouraging creativity and the development of artistic skills, we not only enable individuals to pursue fulfilling careers but also contribute to the overall economic successfulness of a community or a nation. The boost of creativity and the development of artistic skills at all ages have numerous benefits, both at the individual and societal level. The promotion of creativity can lead to the exploration and dissemination of diverse perspectives, fostering inclusivity and understanding. Engaging in creative activities can also provide personal and psychological benefits, such as reducing strain and enhancing well-being. Creativity and artistic development are linked to cognitive growth, fostering critical thinking and problem-solving skills. By encouraging prowess, we can also uncover and nurture endowment, potentially leading to future careers and lifelong hobbies. Creativity and artistic development can contribute to economic growth and innovation, fueling job creation and stimulating entrepreneurship. It is crucial to create an environment that values and supports creativity and artistic development at all ages, recognizing their profound effect on individuals and society as a whole.

IV. SOCIETAL PROGRESS

As an individual become more creative and develops their artistic skills, they inevitably contribute to the progress and enrichment of society as a totally. Creativity has the power to challenge and disrupt established norm, sparking innovation and fostering new idea. Artists, in particular, often use their talent to shed illumination on social issue and injustice, pushing society towards positive change. One path in which creativity and artistic development contribute to societal progress is through the exploration and manifestation of diverse perspective. Through art, individual can deal their unique experience, culture, and belief, offering a glance into world that may be vastly different from our own. This interchange of perspective cultivate empathy, pity, and understanding among masses from diverse background, fostering a more inclusive and tolerant society. By breaking down barrier and bridging gap between different community, art promotes social cohesiveness and helps build a stronger, more cohesive society. Creativity and artistic development encourage critical thinking and problem-solving skills, vital attribute for societal progress. Artists often tackle complex issue through their operate, forcing viewer to question existing paradigm and consider alternative viewpoint. Artistic creations that challenge the position quo invigorate individual to think critically about the globe around them and to actively seek out solution to pressing societal problem. This character of cognitive participation and analytical thinking is crucial for innovation and progress across all industry and field. Artistic endeavor have the potential to influence public opinion and shape insurance decision. Throughout chronicle, art has served as a powerful instrument for social and political comment. Artistic expression, such as lit, euphony, and visual arts, have the power to evoke strong emotion and provoke thought-provoking discussion. By tackling controversial topic and presenting thought-provoking narrative, artists have the power to shape public opinion and encourage societal change. Artistic creations often serve as an accelerator for public discussion and argument, raising consciousness and mobilizing community around pertinent issue. This collective militarization is essential for achieving societal progress and affecting positive change. Creativity and artistic development contribute to economic growth and technological advancement. In the digital years, artistic skills are highly regarded and sought after in various industry. From graphic designer to animator, artists play a significant part in creating visually appealing and engaging substance for consumer. The creative industry, such as movie, style, and ad, generate a billion of dollar in receipts each year, fueling economic growth and task creation. By investing in creativity and artistic development, societies can foster a thriving creative thriftiness and stance themselves at the vanguard of innovation and technological advancement. Creativity and artistic development are essential for societal progress. They promote variety and empathy, foster critical thinking and problem-solving skills, shape public opinion, and contribute to economic growth and technological advancement. Encouraging creativity and the development of artistic skills at all age is crucial for creating a more inclusive, thoughtful, and prosperous society. By supporting and investing in the arts, societies can unleash the transformative power of creativity and pave the path for a bright next.

PROMOTING CULTURAL DIVERSITY AND INCLUSIVITY

Artistic expression has the force to transcend barriers and bring masses together, regardless of their cultural background. By embracing and celebrating diversity, communities can create a thriving surrounding that encourages the exploration of different perspectives and artistic traditions. Inclusivity ensures that everyone has equal access to artistic opportunities, allowing individuals to nurture their creative abilities and contribute to the artistic landscape. It is essential for educational institutions and cultural organizations to establish inclusive practice that promote cultural diversity and ensure that individuals from all backgrounds can participate and contribute to the arts. One path to promote cultural diversity and inclusivity in the arts is through collaborative project that bring together artists from different backgrounds. By facilitating collaboration among artists with diverse cultural perspectives, new artistic expressions and idea can emerge. This not only enriches the artistic procedure but also encourages the exploration and interchange of artistic technique, style, and traditions. Collaboration can be particularly effective in bridging cultural divide and fostering understanding between communities that may have had limited vulnerability to each other's artistic heritage. By working together, artists can create new work that reflect the diverse array of perspectives and experience that exist within a community. Another important facet of promoting cultural diversity and inclusivity is providing equal opportunities for individuals from all backgrounds to engage in the arts. This includes ensuring that art education is accessible to everyone, regardless of their cultural, socioeconomic, or physical characteristic. By offering scholarship, grant, and other form of financial supporting, educational institutions and cultural organizations can help individuals overcome financial barriers and pursue their artistic passion. It is crucial to provide resource and supporting to artists with disability, ensuring that they have the necessary accommodation to fully participate in artistic activity. By removing these barriers, communities can embrace the talent and contribution of individuals from all walk of lifetime, enriching the artistic landscape with diverse voice and perspectives. Promoting cultural diversity and inclusivity in the arts requires the celebration and acknowledgment of different artistic traditions and style. This can be achieved through the organization of multicultural festival, exhibition, and performance that showcase the magnificence and diversity of artistic expressions. By actively promoting and preserving cultural heritage, individuals are encouraged to explore their own cultural root and draw aspiration from their heritage. This not only fosters a feel of congratulate and belong but also encourages the interchange and admiration of different artistic traditions. By recognizing to valuate of diverse artistic expressions, communities can move towards a more inclusive and equitable artistic landscape. Promoting cultural diversity and inclusivity is essential for fostering creativity and artistic development at all ages. By embracing and celebrating diversity, communities provide individuals with opportunities to explore different perspectives and artistic traditions while ensuring equal access to artistic opportunities. Collaborative project, equal opportunities, and the celebration of diverse artistic expressions all contribute to creating an inclusive artistic

landscape. By implementing these practice, educational institutions and cultural organizations can nurture the creative abilities
of individuals from all backgrounds and cultivate a thriving and
vibrant artistic community. A dedication to cultural diversity and
inclusivity in the arts ensures that creativity has no boundary
and that everyone can contribute to and benefit from the artistic
procedure.

ARTISTIC EXPRESSION AS A REFLECTION OF DIVERSE CULTURES

Artistic expression serves as an invaluable tool for reflecting the diversity of cultures around the globe. Through various forms of art, such as paint, sculpt, dancing, and music, individuals are able to express their unique experiences, traditions, and beliefs. These artistic Creation not only provide insight into different cultures but also foster a greater appreciation and understanding of the vast array of human experiences. Artistic representations of diverse cultures allow individuals to explore and connect with unfamiliar perspectives, broadening their horizon and promoting cultural awareness. By showcasing the richness and complexity of different societies, artistic expression encourages the festivity of diversity and serves as an accelerator for cultural interchange and dialogue. In the kingdom of visual humanities, diverse cultures are often depicted through distinctive styles, motif, and subject. Renascence art in EU portrays religious theme, often featuring biblical narrative and Christian symbolization. In contrast, African art is characterized by its vivacious color, abstract forms, and representations of ancestral spirit. By examining these varied artistic styles, one can gain a deeper understanding of the cultural value and beliefs that inform them. The intricate geometrical pattern found in Islamic art reflect the meaning of geometry and math in Islamic fellowship, while Japanese Unicode print reflect the flourishing urban culture during the Tokyo point. Through the survey and appreciation of these diverse artistic expressions, individuals are able to develop a more nuanced understanding of different cultures and their unique perspectives. Dancing and music also play crucial role in the reflection of diverse cultures. Traditional dance, such as the flamenco in Spain or the Bharatanatyam in Bharat, provide a visual representation of cultural individuality and inheritance. These dance often incorporate gesture, movement, and costume that are deeply rooted in the traditions and value of their respective cultures. Similarly, music act as a powerful tool for cultural expression, with each culture possessing its own distinct styles and instrument. The rhythmic beat and melodic tone of African drumming reflect the vibrant vitality and communal liveliness of African societies. In contrast, the intricate harmony and instrumentation of Western classical music reflect the regulate of European cultural traditions. By experiencing and appreciating diverse dancing and music forms, individuals are able to tap into the rich tapes of human artistic expression and develop a greater sensitiveness towards cultural diversity. The internalization of diverse artistic expressions in educational curricula plays a vital role in fostering cultural awareness and promoting inclusivity. By exposing students to art forms from different cultures, educational institute produce opportunity for students to engage with diverse perspectives and challenge their own preconceived notion. This vulnerability not only allows students to appreciate the stunner and singularity of different cultures but also encourages empathy and understanding. By learning about and connecting with different artistic traditions, students are equipped with the necessary tools to engage in meaningful intercultural dialogue and recognize the inherent valuate and contribution of all cultures. This education in artistic diversity then becomes a powerful tool for promoting social justice and equivalence, as students become advocate for inclusivity and regard for all cultural expressions. Artistic expression serves as a reflection of diverse cultures, providing a windowpane into the vast array of human experiences, traditions, and beliefs. Through various art forms, individuals can express and convey their cultural inheritance, often resulting in a greater appreciation and understanding of different societies. By showcasing the richness and complexity of cultural diversity, artistic expression promotes cultural awareness, celebrates divergence, and encourages dialogue and interchange. By incorporating diverse artistic expressions in educational curricula, institution foster cultural awareness and inclusivity, equipping students with the necessary tools to engage with diverse perspectives and promote social justice. In this path, artistic expression plays a crucial role in shaping a more inclusive and culturally diverse fellowship.

ENCOURAGING ARTISTIC SKILLS TO BRIDGE CULTURAL GAPS

Art has the ability to transcend language barriers and evoke emotions that are universal to all individuals, regardless of their background. By promoting artistic development, we are fostering an environment that encourages cultural exchange and understand. This can be particularly relevant in now's globalized globe, where cultural variety is becoming increasingly prevalent. Artistic expression allows individuals to communicate their thinking, feeling, and experience in a non-verbal way. This form of communicating is particularly significant when engaging with individuals from different cultural backgrounds. Through various art forms such as music, dancing, paint, and sculpt, individuals can convey their unique cultural inheritance and tradition. By encouraging the development of artistic skills, we are providing a platform for individuals to showcase their cultural identity and deal their story. Artistic skills can serve as a bridgework between different cultures by providing a common ground for cultural exchange. Artistic collaboration between individuals from different backgrounds can lead to the innovation of unique and innovative work that blend diverse artistic style and technique. This collaboration not only foster a feel of comradery between artist but also promote cultural understand and admiration. By encouraging artist from different cultural backgrounds to collaborate, we can create an environment that celebrates variety and promotes cultural exchange. Artistic skills can also play a significant part in challenging cultural stereotype and prejudice. By encouraging individuals to develop their artistic skills, we are providing them with a platform to challenge preconceived notion about different cultures. Through their art, individuals can showcase alternative narrative that challenge stereotypical representation. This can help break down cultural barriers and foster a more inclusive and tolerant fellowship. Artistic expression can serve as an accelerator for initiating conversations about social issues and global challenge. Artist have a unique ability to provoke think and invigorate activity through their Creation. By encouraging artistic skills, we are empowering individuals to use their art as an intermediate for social change. Whether it is through visual art, music, or execution, artist can use their skills to address issues such as impoverishment, favoritism, or environmental debasement. Through their art, individuals can raise consciousness, invigorate empathy, and incite others to take activity. In plus, promoting artistic skills can have significant economic benefit. The creative manufacture is a booming sphere that contributes to economic growth and task innovation. By encouraging individuals to develop their artistic skills, we are nurturing a pond of endowment that can contribute to this manufacture. Whether it is through designing, performing, or selling art, individuals with artistic skills can find employ opportunity in various creative fields. This can, in turning, contribute to economic development and cultural enrichment. Encouraging artistic skills can be a powerful tool in bridging cultural gaps. Artistic expression has the ability to transcend language barriers and evoke emotions that are universal to all individuals. By promoting artistic development, we are fostering an environment that encourages cultural exchange, challenge stereotype, initiate conversations about social issues, and contributes to economic growth. By recognizing the grandness of artistic skills in the development of individuals and society, we can create a more inclusive and harmonious globe.

FOSTERING EMPATHY AND UNDERSTANDING

Through engaging with art, individuals are able to step into the shoes of others and gain a deeper understanding of different perspectives and experiences. Art has the force to evoke emotions and elicit empathy by providing a tangible theatrical of the human condition. By exploring theme such as societal issues, personal struggle, and cultural variety, art invites individuals to reflect on their own belief and value. This contemplation encourages empathy as individuals recognize the shared experiences and emotions that connect all humankind. Art can challenge stereotypes and prejudices by showcasing alternative narrative and marginalized voice. Artist have historically used their creativity to address social injustice, bring consciousness to important cause, and promote social alter. Through their operate, they highlight the often-overlooked experiences of marginalized community, fostering empathy and understanding in those who engage with their art. Art provides a program for dialog and communicating. Whether it is through visual humanities, euphony, or dramaturgy, art bring masses together and creates an infinite for open discourse and interchange of ideas. This enables individuals to engage in meaningful conversation and develop a deeper admiration for variety and different perspectives. By actively participating in artistic activities, individuals become more attuned to the experiences of others and develop the ability to understand and respect diverse viewpoint. Art encourage active listen, as individuals engage with diverse voice and ideas. Through this procedure, empathy flourish as individuals develop the capability to listen and resonate with the emotions and experiences of others. Fostering empathy and understanding through art has numerous benefits beyond the individual level. As society become increasingly diverse and interconnected, the ability to appreciate and understand different perspectives becomes essential for social cohesion and concord. Art allows individuals to transcend cultural, linguistic, and social barrier and link with others on a deeper level. This promotes intercultural understanding and helps to break down stereotypes and prejudices. By exposing individuals to different cultural tradition, artistic expressions, and narrative, art foster a feel of global citizenship and encourages individuals to embrace variety. This, in turning, contributes to the development of inclusive and compassionate society. Fostering empathy and understanding through art has significance for the teaching scheme. Art program in school not only nurture creativity and artistic skill but also cultivate empathy and social skill. By engaging in artistic activities, student are encouraged to step into the shoes of others and explore different perspectives, promoting empathy and understanding. Art also encourages collaboration and teamwork, as student work together to create meaningful artistic expressions. This skill are invaluable in a rapidly changing globe where individuals need to collaborate and empathize with others from diverse background. Fostering empathy and understanding through art prepare individuals for active and engaged citizenship. By developing the ability to understand and appreciate different viewpoint, individuals are better equipped to contribute to their community and speech important societal issues. Fostering empathy and understanding is a vital facet of creativity and artistic development. Through engaging with art, individuals gain a deeper understanding of the human condition, challenge stereotypes, and develop the ability to listen and resonate with the experiences of others. Fostering empathy and understanding through art has numerous benefits, both at the individual and societal level. It promotes social cohesion, intercultural understanding, and the development of pity and inclusive community. It equips individuals with the skill necessary for active and engaged citizenship in a diverse and interconnected globe.

ARTISTIC EXPERIENCES PROMOTING EMPATHY TOWARDS OTHERS

Through various artistic mediums, individuals are able to step into the shoes of others, gaining a deeper understanding and admiration for their experiences and emotions. Visual arts, Allow artist to portray the emotions and struggle of different individuals or group, thereby fostering empathy in the audience. Painting, sculpture, and photograph can capture the gist of a minute, conveying the joy, sorrow, and challenge that others face. By engaging with this artwork, viewer can develop a sense of empathy, as they immerse themselves in the depicted situation. Similarly, performing arts, such as theater, dancing, and euphony, provide opportunities for both performer and audiences to experience the emotions and perspectives of others. In theater, actor take on the role of characters from various background, sharing their story and shedding light on their struggle, hope, and dream. This procedure requires performer to deeply connect with their characters, empathizing with their experiences in ordering to portray them authentically. Similarly, audiences are invited to identify with and understand these characters, creating a shared experience that promotes empathy and pity. Dancing, with its expressive movement and gesture, can convey an array of emotions without the want for phrase. This form of artistic expression transcend words barrier, connecting individuals on a deeper tier through the power of drift and the raw emotions it evokes. Euphony, too, has the power to foster empathy by stirring the emotions of listener. Whether through lyric, melody, or rhythm, euphony can transport individuals to

different world, evoking an innumerable of emotions and enabling them to better understand the experiences of others. By
engaging in artistic experiences, individuals are provided with a
unique chance to step outside their own perspectives and immerse themselves in the experiences of others. In addition to
promoting empathy towards others, artistic experiences also
encourage a sense of connection and community. By engaging
with art, individuals are able to find common soil with others,
fostering a sense of belonging and understanding. Artistic endeavor often brings masses together, whether it be through collaborative project or shared experiences. Creative community
provide an infinite for individuals to not only express themselves, but to also connect with others who may have similar
experiences or interest. This sense of connection and community
is particularly important in a fellowship that often feels frag-
mented and divided. Artistic experiences provide a program for
individuals to come together, bridging divide and fostering a
sense of empathy and understanding. Artistic experiences can
also serve as a catalyst for social change and activism. Through
various artistic mediums, individuals can shed light on important
social issue, promoting empathy and encouraging others to take
activity. Art has a unique power to communicate complex idea
and emotions in a path that transcends traditional boundary,
allowing individuals to connect with others from different background and perspectives. Whether it be through visual arts, performing arts, or any other form of expression, artistic experiences have the potential to foster empathy towards others, promote a sense of connection and community, and inspire positive
change in the world. Artistic experiences are a vital tool in pro-

moting empathy towards others. Through various artistic mediums, individuals are able to step into the shoes of others, gaining a deeper understanding of their experiences and emotions.
Visual arts, performing arts, and other form of expression provide opportunities for artist and audiences alike to connect with
and empathize with different perspectives. In addition to promoting empathy, artistic experiences also foster a sense of connection and community, bringing individuals together and encouraging a sense of belonging and understanding. Artistic experiences have the power to inspire positive change and serve
as a catalyst for social activism. By engaging in artistic experiences, individuals can develop a greater sense of empathy towards others, promote a sense of connection and community,
and lend to a more empathetic and understanding world.

ART AS A MEDIUM FOR SOCIAL COMMENTARY AND CHANGE

Throughout chronicle, artists have used their creativity and artistic skills to express their view on pressing social issues and provoke public discourse. One such example is the art drift known as Dada, which emerged in the early 20th hundred as a reaction to the horror of World warfare I. Zappa artists rejected traditional form of art and embraced nonsensical and irrational element as a way to criticize the pointlessness of warfare and the fellowship that had allowed it to happen. Artists such as Marcel Duchamp and Hannah Hoc created provocative work that challenged prevailing notion of stunner and reasonableness, forcing viewers to question the position quo and consider alternative way of thinking and living. In more recent days, artists have continued to use their work to shine an illumination on social injustices and bring attention to marginalized community. One notable example is the street artist known as Banksy, whose politically charged and often controversial artwork have gained worldwide attention. Banksy's stenciled graffito artwork, which often depict political and social theme, have been showcased in various cities around the world and have sparked important conversation about topic such as immigration, impoverishment, and administration surveillance. By using public space as his canvass, Banksy ensures that his art is accessible to a wide interview and does not remain confined within the wall of traditional gallery. His work serves as a reminder that art has the power to disrupt and challenge established systems, and that it can be used as an instrument for social change. Art has the ability to humanize issues and create empathy among viewers. One example of this is the 1987 aid monument Quilt, which was created as a way to honor and remember those who had died from AIDS-related illness. The quilt, which consists of thousands of individual panel created by friend and kinfolk member of those affected by aid, served as a powerful symbolization of the devastating affect of the epidemic and the humankind of those affected by it. Viewing the quilt, with its personal story and artistic expression, allowed the populace to connect with the individual lives that had been lost, fostering empathy and understanding for a marginalized community. This example demonstrates how art has the capability to transcend mere phrase and statistic, and can touch masses on an emotional tier, motivating them to take activity and consequence change. In plus to its power to create empathy and provoke thought, art also has the ability to offer imaginative solutions to complex social problems. Through their work, artists can propose alternative vision of fellowship and inspire others to envision a better world. This can be seen in the work of the designer and visionary Buck minster total. Total believed that designing and engineering could solve many of the world's problems, such as impoverishment and environmental debasement. Through his innovative design, such as the geodesic attic, total challenged conventional thinking and offered new possibility for sustainable living. His work continues to inspire designer, architect, and environmentalist now, serving as a reminder that through creativity and imitativeness, we can find solutions to pressing societal issues. Art serves as a powerful medium for social commentary and change. Artists throughout chronicle have used their creative ability to challenge prevailing belief, bring attention to social injustices, create empathy, and propose imaginative solutions to complex problems. The example discussed in this paragraph demonstrate how art has the potential to disrupt established systems, create empathy among viewers, and inspire individual to envision and work towards a better world. Encouraging creativity and the developing of artistic skills in individual of all age can therefore play a vital part in fostering social consciousness, empathy, and positive change. Creativity is a vital facet of human development that plays a significant role in fostering artistic skills at all ages. By encouraging creativity and artistic development, individuals can unlock their full possible, explore new ideas, and express themselves in unique and innovative way. In today's rapidly changing world, where the ability to think outside the corner and adjust to new challenge is crucial, nurturing creativity becomes even more essential. Whether it is through painting, writing, or performing, engaging in artistic activities can have a profound impact on individuals' cognitive, emotional, and social development. One of the key benefit of encouraging creativity and artistic development at all ages is its positive impact on cognitive abilities. Engaging in artistic activities stimulates various regions of the psyche, fostering the development of critical think, problem-solving, and analytical skills. Creating a slice of art requires individuals to think creatively, program, and organize their ideas in a lucid and visually appealing way. This procedure not only enhances individuals' cognitive abilities but also improves their remembering and care bridge. When individuals engage in artistic activities, they are often required to make decision, evaluate different option, and find innovative solution to artistic challenge. This not only helps develop their cognitive tractability but also strengthens their ability to think critically and creatively in different context. Fostering creativity and artistic development also has a significant impact on individuals' emotional well-being. Artistic activities provide individuals with a mean to express their emotion, thinking, and experience, allowing them to gain a deeper understand of themselves and the world around them. Whether it is through painting, writing, or performing, artistic endeavors provide individuals with a vent to express their feeling and emotion that may be difficult to articulate verbally. This can ultimately lead to a sense of duration and emotional publish, reducing strain and promoting overall psychological well-being. Participation in artistic activities has been found to improve individuals' self-esteem and self-confidence. Creating something unique and beautiful instill a sense of congratulate and achievement, boosting individuals' trust in their abilities and fostering a positive self-image. In plus to its cognitive and emotional benefit, encouraging creativity and artistic development at all ages also plays a crucial role in fostering social connections and promoting cultural exchange. Artistic activities often require individuals to collaborate and communicate with others, fostering teamwork, empathy, and effective communicating skills. Participating in a dramaturgy output necessitates coordination and cooperation among actor, director, and other member of the output squad. This collaborative nature of artistic endeavors provides individuals with opportunity to understand different perspective, negotiate contradictory ideas, and operate towards a common finish. Artistic activities can also serve as a program for cultural exchange, allowing individuals to deal their unique experience and tradition with others. In this path, artistic manifestation becomes a powerful instrument for fostering empathy, understanding, and admiration for diverse culture and perspective. Encouraging creativity and the development of artistic skills at all ages is crucial for promoting cognitive, emotional, and social well-being. The ability to think creatively and express oneself artistically is essential in today's rapidly changing world, where adaptability and invention are highly valued. By engaging in artistic activities, individuals can enhance their cognitive abilities, improve emotional well-being, and foster social connections. It is vital to provide individuals with the necessary resource and supporting to explore their creative possible and engage in artistic endeavors throughout their life.

V. EARLY CHILDHOOD

In the early childhood stage, children begin to develop their creative and artistic skills in a more structured and formal way. This is the time when they start to explore their imagination and learn to express themselves through various art forms. One key facet of early childhood creativity is the development of fine motor skills. As children engage in activities such as draw, color, and paint, they are not only learning to hold and control art material but also strengthening their hand-eye coordination. This enhances their ability to manipulate tool, which is crucial for future artistic endeavors. Early childhood is a point marked by immense oddity and a sense of question. Children at this stage are constantly observing their environs, asking question, and experimenting with their surroundings. This natural tendency towards exploration and experiment foster creativity and allows children to cultivate their artistic sensibility. Early childhood is a time when children are exposed to diverse art forms and medium. They encounter euphony, dancing, play, and visual humanities, which provide them with a rich array of creative opportunity. By engaging in these different art forms, children can discover their interest and aptitude, and even find their true love. Early childhood creativity is not only limited to traditional art forms but encompass everyday activities as well. Children at this stage engage in imaginative run, storytelling, and role-playing, all of which contribute to their creative development. These activities allow children to create their own narrative, invent character, and explore various perspectives, which are essential skills for artistic manifestation. Early childhood creativity extends beyond personal manifestation and fosters the development of social and emotional skills. Through art activities, children learn to collaborate, convey, and empathize with others. They engage in grouping project, deal idea, and appreciate different perspectives. This not only enhances their creativity but also builds their capability to work collaboratively and resolve conflict. Early childhood creativity plays a vital part in cognitive development. Art activities require children to think critically, make decision, and solve problem. When children engage in artistic endeavors, they are constantly making choice about color, shape, and composition. They learn to experiment with different material and technique, testing their own idea and concept. This procedure of tribulation and mistake stimulates their analytical think and problem-solving skills. It also strengthens their ability to think creatively and approach task from multiple perspectives. Early childhood creativity has a profound effect on the overall development of children. Inquiry has shown that engagement in creative activities can enhance children's self-confidence, self-esteem, and tenacity. As children engage in artistic endeavors, they learn to take risk, make mistake, and remain in to confront of challenge. They develop a sense of achievement and congratulate in their operate, which contributes to their overall well-being. Early childhood creativity provides children with a mean of self-expression and a path to make sense of their emotion. Through art, children can communicate their thinking, feeling, and experience, even when they may not have the phrase to express themselves verbally. They learn to express their delight, sorrow, and ire, fostering emotional regulating and resiliency. Early childhood is a critical time for the development of creativity and artistic skills. Through various art forms, children refine their fine motor skills, explore their imagination, and express themselves. Early childhood creativity not only enhances cognitive development but also foster social and emotional skills. Engagement in creative activities promotes self-confidence, self-esteem, and emotional well-being. It is crucial to encourage and support creativity at an early age to ensure the holistic development of children.

EARLY EXPOSURE TO CREATIVITY AND ART

Creativity and artistic development are essential aspects of overall cognitive, emotional, and social increase. The importance of early exposure to creativity and art cannot be overstated as it provides children with a fundamental groundwork for their future artistic endeavors. In the early days of lifetime, children have an innate oddity and keenness to explore their environs. This oddity should be nurtured and encouraged through various forms of artistic expression, including draw, paint, euphony, and dancing. Through these activities, children develop their fine centrifugal skills, spatial consciousness, and creativity. Early exposure to creativity and art can enhance the child's cognitive abilities, including problem-solving, critical think, and decision-making skills. By engaging in creative activities, children learn to think outside the corner and develop innovative approach to challenge, which are crucial skills in various discipline and careers. Art provides a unique boulevard for emotional expression and self-discovery. When children create art, they have the exemption to express their emotions, thinking, and experience in a non-verbal and non-judgmental path. This procedure allows them to develop a sense of self-identity and explore their emotions in a safe and supportive surroundings. Artistic expression can foster social connections and communication skills. Participating in art class or collaborative artistic project enables children to interact with others, deal idea, and collaborate on creative endeavors. This social interaction helps children develop empathy, communication skills, and an appreciation for diverse perspectives. These skills are vital for building

meaningful relationship and navigating social situation throughout lifetime. In plus to personal increase, early exposure to creativity and art also contributes to cultural appreciation and consciousness. Art is a powerful instrument for exploring different
cultures, historical period, and social issue. By exposing children
to diverse forms of artistic expression, they develop an understanding and regard for different cultures and perspectives. This
increased cultural consciousness leads to a more inclusive and
empathetic fellowship. Early exposure to creativity and art can
have long-term benefit for individual pursuing careers in the
arts. By providing children with the chance to engage in various
artistic activities, they can discover their love and develop their
artistic skills. This early exposure also helps children build a
strong groundwork in artistic technique, aesthetic, and art
chronicle. Such early preparation can set the phase for future
achiever and provide a head begin in pursuing further teaching
or a career in the arts. Early exposure to creativity and art can
also have a positive effect on overall well-being. Engaging in
creative activities has been shown to reduce strain, encourage
loosening, and improve overall mental health. The procedure of
creating art has a therapeutic consequence, allowing individual
to focus their care, reduce anxiousness, and gain a sense of
achievement. Artistic expression has been used as a form of
therapy to support individual with mental health challenge and
encourage heal. The importance of early exposure to creativity
and art is significant in many aspects of human development.
By providing children with opportunity for artistic expression,
they can develop essential cognitive, emotional, and social
skills. Early exposure to creativity and art enhance cognitive

abilities, supports emotional expression and self-discovery, foster social connections, and promotes cultural appreciation. It can lay the foundation for future careers in the arts and lend to overall well-being. It is crucial for educator, parent, and community to prioritize and encourage early exposure to creativity and art as a fundamental aspect of human increase and development.

EARLY CHILDHOOD AS A CRITICAL PERIOD FOR BRAIN DEVELOPMENT

During this phase, the brain undergoes rapid increase and shakeup, forming the foundation for learning, behavior, and health later in lifetime. The developing brain is highly responsive to environmental influences and experiences, making this period a prime chance to stimulate and nurture cognitive, emotional, and social development. Inquiry has shown that early experiences and interactions have a profound impact on the architecture of the brain, shaping its construction and operate. Vulnerability to a rich and stimulating environment during this critical period can enhance synaptic connection, promote the development of neural pathway, and optimize the brain's overall function. On the other paw, adverse experiences, such as negligence or maltreatment, can have detrimental effects on brain development, leading to long-lasting cognitive, emotional, and behavioral impairment. This underscores the importance of providing children with positive, nurturing, and stimulating environments in their earliest days to lay the foundation for healthy brain development and subsequent thriving. This critical period is marked by heightened plasticity, meaning that the brain is more malleable and responsive to experiences and interventions. Early childhood presents a unique window of chance where interventions and interventions can have a significant impact on shaping the developing brain. Inquiry has shown that early stimulation and enrichment program, such as high-quality preschool teaching, can have long-term positive effects on a child's cognitive abilities, language skills, and schooling preparedness. Early interventions for developmental delays, learning disabilities, or behavioral problem can be highly effective during this critical period, as the brain is more receptive to change and interventions. This highlights the importance of early identification and intervention for children who may be at danger for developmental delays or disabilities, as timely interventions can significantly improve outcome and mitigate potential long-term consequence. Early childhood is a clock of rapid language development, with children acquiring language skills at an astonishing tempo. The brain's plasticity and receptivity to acquiring language during this period make it an optimal clock for linguistic stimulation and language learning. Vulnerability to rich and varied language comment, such as reading to children, engaging in conversation, and providing language-rich environments, can greatly facilitate language development and lay the foundation for strong literacy skills. This has significant significance for educational achiever later in lifetime, as language and literacy skills are essential for academic accomplishment and social-emotional well-being. Early childhood is a critical period for the development of social-emotional skills and self-regulation. During this clock, children are acquiring vital social and emotional competence, such as empathy, emotional regulating, and dispute resolving. The caliber of early relationship and interactions, such as safe attachment with caregiver and positive equal relationship, plays a crucial part in fostering social-emotional development. Interventions that promote social-emotional learning and positive equal interactions during early childhood can have lasting effects on emotional well-being, mental health, and social function in later days. Early childhood is a critical period for brain development, wherein the brain is highly responsive to environmental influences, experiences, and interventions. Positive and enriching experiences during this period can optimize brain development, while adverse experiences can have detrimental effects. The heightened plasticity and receptivity of the developing brain during early childhood introduce a unique window of chance for interventions and interventions that can shape the brain's architecture and set the phase for later learning, behavior, and health. Providing children with nurture and stimulating environments, early identification and intervention for developmental delays, and opportunity for language and social-emotional development are crucial for supporting optimal brain development in early childhood.

ARTISTIC ACTIVITIES PROMOTING FINE MOTOR SKILLS AND COORDINATION

Fine motor skills refer to the intricate movements performed with the small muscles of the hands and finger, which are essential for activities such as write, drawing, painting, and playing musical instrument. Similarly, coordination involves the integrating of torso movements in a smooth and efficient way. By engaging in artistic activities, individuals are able to enhance their fine motor skills and coordination through various means. One path in which artistic activities promote fine motor skills and coordination is through to utilize of different art medium. Painting with brush of varying size and thickness requires individuals to grasp the brush properly and control their hand and finger movements to create precise stroke. This not only strengthens the muscles in the hand and finger but also improves hand-eye coordination as individuals focus on guiding the brush to create the desired consequence on the canvass. Similarly, molding mud or sculpting requires individuals to manipulate their hands and finger to shape the stuff into specific form, which further enhances their fine motor skills and coordination. Artistic activities that involve drawing or sketching allow individuals to refine their fine motor skills and coordination. Whether using pencil, pen, or other drawing tools, individuals are required to exert control over their hand and finger movements to produce accurate line, curve, and shape. As they continue to exercise, their fine motor skills improve, enabling them to create more intricate and detailed art. The preciseness required in drawing helps individuals develop better hand-eye co-ordination, as they learn to observe their subject and translate the visual info onto newspaper. Another facet of artistic activities that contribute to the development of fine motor skills and coordination is the act of manipulating various material. Cutting and pasting different shape and texture in collage-making requires individuals to use scissor or other cut tools, as well as paste or adhesive. These activities necessitate precise hand movements to achieve the desired result. Similarly, stringing bead to create jewelry or weaving fiber on a predominate requirements individuals to manipulate their finger and hands with sleight, promoting fine motor skills and coordination. Engaging in these tactile experience enhances individuals' power to control their hand movements, facilitating the subtlety of fine motor skills. In plus to the physical aspect, artistic activities also promote fine motor skills and coordination through cognitive engagement. Artistic endeavor often requires individuals to plan, strategize, and execute their ideas, thus stimulating their cognitive and problem-solving ability. When engaging in activities such as drawing, painting, or sculpting, individuals must consider makeup, coloration concord, and spatial relationship, among other element. This cognitive engagement contributes to the development of fine motor skills and coordination, as individuals learn to translate their ideas into physical form while attending to detail and aesthetic consideration. Artistic activities provide individuals with opportunity to develop and enhance their fine motor skills and coordination. By engaging in various art form and medium, individuals are able to refine their hand and finger movements, strengthening the muscles involved and improving hand-eye coordination. Manipulating different material and engaging in cognitive process such as plan and problem-solving further facilitate the development of fine motor skills and coordination. Incorporating artistic activities into single's lifetime at any age can be highly beneficial, not just for creative manifestation but also for the holistic development of fine motor skills and coordination.

ENCOURAGING PLAY-BASED LEARNING AND IMAGINATION

Play is essential for the development of cognitive, physical, and social skills, and it provides a fertile soil for nurturing imagination and creativity. By engaging in play, individuals can explore different role, experiment with ideas, and create their own narrative. Play-based learning also allows individuals to learn through tribulation and mistake, foster problem-solving skills, and develop a sense of oddity and exploration. Imagination is a powerful instrument for creativity and artistic expression. It allows individuals to envision possibility beyond the boundary of realism and to bring those vision to lifetime through various artistic medium. By encouraging imagination, individuals are able to tap into their inner creativity and explore new ideas, perspectives, and concept. This is particularly relevant in the humanities, where artist often draw aspiration from their imagination to create unique and innovative work. One way to encourage play-based learning and imagination is by providing open-ended materials and environment that allow individuals to freely explore and create. In early puerility education, providing child with ample opportunity to engage in pretend play with prop and materials can stimulate their imagination and encourage storytelling. Such practice allow young child to make sense of the surrounding globe, express their thinking and emotion, and develop their imagination. Similarly, in higher education, providing students with creative space, such as art studio or collaborative workspace, can foster play-based learning and imagination.

These space allow students to experiment with different materials, technique, and ideas, and to freely express their creativity without opinion or constraint. Another way to encourage play-based learning and imagination is by incorporating play elements and activity into the curriculum. Teacher can design games and interactive exercise that require students to think creatively, problem-solve, and imagine new possibility. By incorporating play into the learning procedure, students are more likely to stay engaged and motivated, and to develop a deeper understand of the subject issue. Play-based learning encourages students to think critically and independently, as they are required to come up with their own ideas and solution. In plus to providing open-ended materials and incorporating play elements into the curriculum, educators can also encourage play-based learning and imagination by fostering a supportive and non-judgmental surroundings. When individuals feel safe to take risk, make mistake, and explore new ideas, they are more likely to engage in creative and imaginative activity. Educators play a vital part in creating such an surrounding by valuing and acknowledging diverse perspectives, celebrating creativity and imagination, and providing constructive feedback that encourages increase and exploration. Technology can be used to support play-based learning and imagination. Digital tool, such as interactive games and virtual realism, can provide individuals with immersive and engaging experience that stimulate their imagination and creativity. Technology can be used to connect individuals from different background and culture, allowing them to collaborate and exchange ideas, and inspiring new form of artistic expression. Encouraging play-based learning and imagination is instrumental in fostering creativity and artistic development. Play allows individuals to explore, experiment, and create, while imagination provides the fire for creative expression. By providing open-ended materials and environment, incorporating play elements into the curriculum, fostering a supportive surrounding, and utilizing technology, educators can create opportunity for individuals of all ages to engage in play-based learning and unleash their imaginative possible. By embracing play and imagination, individuals can develop their creative skills, enhance their artistic expression, and enrich their life.

PLAY AS A FOUNDATION FOR CREATIVITY AND ARTISTIC DEVELOPMENT

Through play, children engage in imaginative and creative activities that foster their artistic abilities and enhance their cognitive and sensory skills. Play allows children to explore their environs, experiment with various materials, and express themselves freely. This unrestricted exploration not only stimulates their artistic development but also nurtures their creativity and problem-solving abilities. When children engage in feign play, they use their imitativeness to create fictional scenario, character, and storyline. This imaginative play not only allows them to express themselves but also challenges them to think critically and problem resolve as they navigate through their invented globe. Play often involves to utilize of various art materials, such as crayon, paint, and mud, enabling children to experiment with different medium and develop their artistic skills. The tactile feel of manipulating these materials enhances their sensorial development, coordination, and fine centrifugal skills. Play provides children with a program to express their emotions, thinking, and experience in a creative and constructive way. By engaging in various forms of play, such as draw, storytelling, or drama, children can communicate their feeling and ideas, gaining a sense of self-expression and authorization. By encouraging play, parents, educators, and caregivers can foster a child's creativity and artistic development, laying the foundation for a life of artistic exploration and manifestation. Play promotes holistic development and enhances various cognitive, emotional, and social skills. Participating in creative activities during playtime stimulates children's cognitive development by challenging their problem-solving abilities, critical think skills, and spatial consciousness. When constructing a hulk with construction block, children must conceptualize the designing, plan their action, and develop strategy to overcome any challenge. Through this procedure, they learn to approach problem analytically and develop their logical reason skills. Play engages children emotionally, allowing them to explore and express their emotions through creative outlet. This emotional exploration foster self-awareness, empathy, and emotional regulating, enhancing their overall emotional news. Play encourage cooperation, communicating, and social interaction, as children often engage in collaborative play with their peer. This social interaction not only supports their social-emotional development but also cultivates important skills such as talks, share, and perspective-taking. By engaging in playful activities that promote artistic manifestation, children develop a heightened sense of empathy and understanding of others' perspective, fostering positive relationship and a sense of belong. Play-based artistic activities have been shown to positively impact academic accomplishment and self-esteem. Study have indicated that integrating humanities teaching into academic curriculum enhances student' overall academic execution. By incorporating art forms such as euphony, drama, and visual humanities into traditional subject, student are encouraged to approach learn in a creative and multisensory way, enhancing their participation and understanding of the material. Engaging in artistic activities during playtime can boost self-esteem and self-confidence. When children are given the exemption to explore their artistic abilities, express their ideas, and receive positive feedback, they develop a sense of achievement and congratulate in their creative achievement. This increased self-esteem not only contributes to their overall well-being but also motivates them to continue exploring and developing their artistic skills. Play serves as a crucial foundation for creativity and artistic development at all age. By engaging in various forms of play, children are able to explore their creative possible, develop their artistic skills, and enhance their cognitive, emotional, and social development. Play provides children with a program for self-expression, problem-solving, and imaginative think, fostering a lifelong admiration for the humanities. By encouraging and embracing play as an essential element of childhood, parents, educators, and caregivers can support the holistic development of children, nurturing their creativity and artistic possible.

IMAGINATIVE PLAY FOSTERING COGNITIVE AND EMOTIONAL GROWTH

From early childhood to adulthood, engaging in imaginative play allows individuals to experiment with new idea, develop problem-solving skills, and explore their emotions in a safe and controlled surroundings. Inquiry has consistently shown that imaginative play has numerous benefits for cognitive development. By creating imaginary scenario and character, individuals are able to practice their creative think and problem-solving abilities. They are encouraged to think outside the corner, come up with unique solution, and consider multiple perspective. This type of cognitive flexibility is essential for navigating the complexity of the modern globe and finding innovative solution to various challenge. Imaginative play also plays a crucial part in emotional growth. Throughout the procedure of engaging in imaginative play, individuals have the opportunity to explore and express their emotions in a safe and non-threatening way. They can experiment with different role and personality, allowing them to understand and navigate their own emotions better as well as those of others. A child may pretend to be a physician, caring for their imaginary patient, which allows them to empathize and understand the feeling of others. This type of play allows individuals to explore different emotional situation, which can be particularly helpful for those who struggle with emotional regulating or have difficulty expressing themselves. It provides a creative vent for emotions that may otherwise be suppressed or misunderstand. Imaginative play encourages individuals to develop their communicating and social skills. When engaging in pretend play, individuals must collaborate, negotiate, and communicate effectively with others to create a lucid and engaging storyline. This type of interaction foster the development of important social skills, such as active listen, turn-taking, and cooperation. In plus, imaginative play often occurs in group, providing individuals with the opportunity to practice skills such as leaders, dispute resolving, and compromise. These skills are not only essential for social and personal relationship but are also highly valued in educational and professional setting. Imaginative play can also have long-lasting effect on artistic development. As individuals engage in imaginative play, they are constantly required to use their creativity and imitativeness to bring their idea to life. This constant exercising of the imitativeness can have a profound impact on artistic skills. Whether it is creating a make-believe globe or designing costume and prop, individuals participating in imaginative play are constantly honing their artistic abilities. They have the opportunity to experiment with different art form, such as draw, paint, and sculpting, to bring their imaginary world to life. This type of creative participation foster artistic trust, allowing individuals to explore their artistic talent and develop a unique artistic flair. Imaginative play is a powerful tool that foster both cognitive and emotional growth in individuals. From early childhood to adulthood, engaging in imaginative play provides numerous benefits, including enhanced cognitive flexibility, improved emotional understand, and the development of important social skills. Imaginative play has a profound impact on artistic development, allowing individuals to hone their creative and artistic abilities. Encouraging and promoting imaginative play at all ages is essential for fostering creativity and artistic development, as well as for personal and social growth. Creativity and artistic development play a crucial role in personal growth and self-expression. Encouraging creativity and the development of artistic skills at all ages is not only beneficial for individual fulfillment but also for societal progress. From a young age, children should be given the opportunity to explore various artistic mediums and engage in creative activity. This fosters their imitativeness and encourages them to think outside the corner. As they grow older, this creativity becomes invaluable as they are able to approach problem with innovative solution. Artistic development allows individuals to communicate their thinking, emotion, and experience in unique and meaningful way. Art can transcend words barrier and express message that phrase alone cannot. It serves as a universal word, connecting masses from different background and culture. Engaging in art can have therapeutic benefit, serving as a form of self-expression and providing a vent for emotion. Encouraging creativity and artistic development throughout a someone's lifetime helps cultivate a well-rounded individual. In the early stage of teaching, stress should be placed on providing a wide array of art experience. This can include exposure to different art forms such as paint, sculpt, euphony, and dramaturgy. By doing so, children have the opportunity to discover their personal interest and talent, while also developing an admiration for various art forms. Art teaching should go beyond simply teaching technique and skills ; it should encourage critical think, problem-solving, and creativity. This can be achieved through project-based learn and open-ended assignment that allow student to express their own unique idea and interpretation. As individuals progress into adolescence and maturity, their creative skills and interest may evolve. It is crucial to continue fostering artistic development during these stage by providing opportunities for further exploration and growth. This can be done through art class, workshop, and community program that offer specialized preparation and exposure to different artistic mediums. Creating a supportive and inclusive surroundings where individuals feel confident to deal their operate and receive constructive feedback is essential. This can be achieved through art club, exhibition, and collaboration with local artist. Encouraging creativity and artistic development at all ages not only benefit individuals but also contributes to societal progress. Art has the power to challenge established norm and provoke discourse on important social issue. By providing a program for diverse voice to be heard, art can bring about positive alter and promote social jurist. Art has the power to inspire, upthrust, and unite communities. It has the power to create a feel of belong and nurture empathy by allowing individuals to connect with others on an emotional tier. Art also contributes to the cultural individuality of a society, preserving tradition and celebrating variety. Creativity and artistic development should be encouraged at all ages. The benefit of engaging in artistic activity and nurturing creative skills are diverse and far-reaching. From personal fulfillment and self-expression to fostering invention, art plays a crucial role in individual and societal growth. By providing opportunities for exploration, learn, and self-expression, individuals can cultivate their artistic talent and contribute to the cultural cloth of their communities. The publicity of creativity and artistic development at all ages ensures that art remains an integral component of our society, inspiring and enriching the life of individuals for generation to come.

VI. SCHOOL YEARS

The school years play a crucial part in the development of creativity and artistic skills. During this point, students are exposed to a wide range of subject and activities that help nurture their creative abilities. Schools have a responsibility to provide a supportive environment where students can explore their interests and develop their artistic talents. One path schools can do this is by offering a variety of art classes and extracurricular activities. Whether it be painting, drawing, sculpt, or photography, these classes provide students with the chance to experiment with different medium and technique, allowing them to discover their unique artistic flair. Art classes also teach students important skills such as reflection, problem-solving, and self-expression, which are applicable across various discipline and aspects of life. In plus to art classes, schools can also incorporate creativity into other academic subject. Teacher can encourage students to think creatively in subject like lit, science, and math. Reading and analyzing work of lit not only allows students to appreciate the stunner of words but also nurtures their imitativeness and power to think outside the corner. In science, students can be encouraged to design and conduct experiment, fostering their oddity and critical think skills. Math, often seen as a rigid and formulaic topic, can be taught in a path that encourages creative problem-solving, helping students develop a deeper understand of mathematical concept. Schools can promote creativity and artistic development by providing opportunities for students to engage in cultural activities and event. Airfield trip to art museum, theater, or euphony performance can expose students to different form of art and cultivate their admiration for the creative endeavor of others. These experience serve as source of aspiration and can broaden students' artistic horizon. Schools can organize talent show, art competition, or play production, allowing students to showcase their skills and talents in a supportive and encouraging environment. Participating in such event not only boosts students' trust but also allows them to develop essential skills such as teamwork, public speak, and effective communicating. It is important for schools to recognize and support the individual artistic interests and talents of their students. Students have diverse abilities and passion, and it is crucial for schools to provide opportunities that cater to a wide range of artistic interests. In doing so, schools can create an inclusive environment where all students feel valued and supported in their creative pursuit. Recognizing and celebrating the unique talents of students can foster a feel of congratulate and accomplishment, encouraging them to continue developing their artistic abilities. The school years are a crucial point for the development of creativity and artistic skills. Schools have a responsibility to provide a supportive environment where students can explore their interests and develop their artistic talents. By offering a variety of art classes and incorporating creativity into other academic subject, schools can nurture students' creativity and help them develop important skills applicable to various aspects of life. Providing opportunities for students to engage in cultural activities and event and recognizing and supporting individual artistic interests and talents are vital in fostering creativity and the development of artistic skills. With the right support and boost, students can unleash their creative possible, leading to personal increase and a bright next.

INTEGRATING ARTS INTO THE CURRICULUM

Integrating arts into the curriculum not only enriches students' educational feel but also promotes the developing of essential skills and competence. By incorporating various art forms into traditional academic subject, school create a multidimensional learn surroundings that foster creativity, critical thinking, and self-expression. One major gain of integrating arts into the curriculum is that it encourages students to engage with learning materials in a more meaningful and personal path. Illustrating scientific concept or exploring historical event through performing arts not only helps students comprehend the subject issue but also enables them to connect emotionally, making the learning feel more memorable and impactful. The arts provide students with opportunity to develop skills that are transferable to other area of their lifetime and future career. As they engage in artistic activity such as paint, dancing, or playing a musical tool, students improve their fine centrifugal skills, hand-eye coordination, and spatial reason. These physical and cognitive ability are essential in numerous profession, including architecture, operation, and engineer. Integrating arts into the curriculum cultivates critical thinking and problem-solving skills. When students engage in artistic process such as brainstorming idea, experimenting with materials, and making decision about artistic element, they learn to think creatively and analytically, seeking alternative solution and embracing multiple perspective. Such skills are vital in now's complex and rapidly changing globe, where the power to adapt, innovate, and solve problem creatively is highly prized. Integrating arts into the curriculum foster self-expression and personal growth. Artistic activity provide students with a program to express their thinking, emotion, and idea freely, thereby enhancing their self-esteem and trust. Engaging in artistic endeavor promotes self-reflection and introspection, allowing students to gain a clear understand of their own identity, belief, and value. This self-awareness is crucial for personal growth and well-being, as it enables individual to make informed decision and navigate lifetime's challenge with resiliency and genuineness. Despite the numerous benefit of integrating arts into the curriculum, there are some challenge that school may face when implementing such program. One common gainsay is the limited resource and funding available for arts education. Due to financial constraint, many school struggles to provide adequate materials, equipment, and qualified teacher for arts class. As a consequence, some students may not have admittance to the artistic education they deserve, hindering their holistic developing. The emphasis on standardized test and academic execution can overshadow the importance of the arts in the curriculum. With the growing emphasis on stanch subject (skill, engineering, engineer, and mathematics) , arts education is often overlooked or marginalized. This narrow focusing on academic accomplishment neglects the broader goal of education, such as fostering creativity, cultural admiration, and personal growth. Despite these challenge, it is crucial for educator, policymakers, and fellowship as a totally to recognize the importance of integrating arts into the curriculum. By providing students with a well-rounded education that encompasses both the science and the arts, we equip them with the cognition, skills, and perspective necessary for achiever in the twenty-first hundred. As renowned education reformist Sir sight Robinson once said, "The arts, science, arts, physical education, language, and math all have equal, central, and pivotal role to play in a balanced, rigorous, and challenging education." "Integrating arts into the curriculum is not only an investing in our students" academic achiever but also in their overall developing as well-rounded individual.

BENEFITS OF ARTS EDUCATION ON ACADEMIC PERFORMANCE

One of the most compelling reasons to incorporate arts education into the academic curriculum is the significant affect it has on academic execution. Numerous studies have revealed a positive correlation between arts education and improved academic accomplishment across various academic discipline. Firstly, engaging in arts activities such as euphony, dancing, and play enhance cognitive developing, particularly in area such as critical thinking, problem-solving, and spatial reason. Through the process of creating and expressing oneself artistically, students are challenged to think critically, analyze situation from multiple perspective, and find innovative solution, skills that are transferable to academic subject such as mathematics, skill, and language arts. Arts education has been shown to improve read and language skills. Studies have found that students who are involved in activities related to the arts prove enhanced verbal and written communicating skills when compared to their peer. The process of interpreting and analyzing artistic work promotes language developing by expanding lexicon, improving inclusion, and fostering effective oral and written manifestation. Engaging in activities such as acting or public speak can boost trust and self-esteem, factor that greatly contribute to academic achiever. Arts education contributes to improved overall academic engagement and motivating. The creative and dynamic nature of arts activities captivates students' concern and provides a refreshing breaking from traditional schoolroom teaching. By offering a diverse array of arts experience, schools can tap into students' intrinsic motivating and cultivate their love for learning. When students are personally invested and actively engaged in their education, they are more likely to excel academically, persist through challenge, and become lifelong learners. The collaborative nature of arts education fosters a feel of belong and community, promoting positive equal relationship and a supportive learning surroundings. Incorporating arts education into schools can also address the unique learning needs of students with diverse learning style, ability, and background. The arts provide alternative avenue for learning and manifestation, allowing students to showcase their talent, build trust, and enhance their self-identity. For students who may struggle with conventional academic approach, arts education offers an inclusive and accessible path to engage with curriculum substance. Studies have shown that arts integrating in classroom benefit students with diverse learning needs, including those with disability and English language learners. By providing a multisensory and creative vent, arts education enables all students to connect with their learning feel, reinforcing their self-efficacy and academic increase. Arts education nurture skills and character that are essential in the 21st-century workforce. With the rapid advancement in engineering and globalization, employer increasingly seek individuals who possess creativity, adaptability, collaboration, and critical thinking ability. Arts education cultivates these skills by encouraging students to explore innovative idea, take risk, and cooperate with others. By integrating arts education into the academic curriculum, schools can develop well-rounded individuals who are not only academically proficient but also possess the essential skills needed to thrive in the modern work. The comprehension of arts education in the academic curriculum offers numerous benefit, including improved academic execution, enhanced language skills, increased engagement and motivating, adjustment for diverse learning needs, and the developing of essential skills for the 21st-century workforce. Arts education foster critical thinking, creativity, self-expression, and collaboration, skills that are vital for students to succeed academically and thrive in their next pursuit. As we recognize the immense benefit that arts education bring to students, it is crucial that educational institution prioritize and invest in the arts as an integral element of a comprehensive and well-rounded education.

ARTISTIC ACTIVITIES ENHANCING OVERALL LEARNING EXPERIENCE

Artistic activities greatly enhance the overall learning experience, regardless of years. Engaging in creative pursuit and artistic expression helps to foster critical thinking, problem-solving skills, and cognitive development. It encourages individuals to think outside the box, explore different perspective, and challenge traditional ways of thinking. Through artistic activities, individuals are able to communicate idea, emotion, and experience in unique and creative ways. This not only enhances their ability to express themselves but also to understand and empathize with others. Engaging in artistic activities allows individuals to develop a sense of self-awareness and self-confidence, as they are able to see their idea and Creation come to lifetime. This can greatly enhance their overall learning and personal growth. Artistic activities also provide individuals with a program to explore cultural diversity and promote social inclusion. By engaging in various art forms, individuals are able to learn about different culture, tradition, and perspective. This fosters a sense of admiration and regard for diversity, as well as the ability to engage in meaningful dialog and collaboration with others. This not only enhances their understanding of the globe but also promotes empathy and social obligation. Engaging in artistic activities can have a positive effect on individuals' mental health and well-being. Artistic expression has been shown to reduce strain, anxiousness, and slump, as it provides a healthy and constructive vent for emotion. It allows individuals to explore and process their thinking and feeling in a creative and non-judgmental way. Artistic activities have been found to improve concentration, focus, and remembering, as individuals are required to pay care to particular, make connection, and analyze info. This can greatly enhance their overall learning experience and academic execution. Engaging in artistic activities promotes self-discipline, perseverance, and a growth mindset. Through the procedure of creating art, individuals learn to embrace challenge, learn from mistake, and remain in the confront of obstacle. This resiliency and decision are transferrable skills that can be applied to other area of their life and lend to their overall personal and professional achiever. Engaging in artistic activities foster innovation and creativeness, which are essential skills in now's rapidly changing globe. By encouraging individuals to think creatively and develop their artistic skills, we are cultivating a civilization of innovation and adaptability. Artistic activities allow individuals to approach problem and challenge from different angle, explore novel solution, and think outside the box. This creative problem-solving is a valuable skill in various discipline and industry, as it enables individuals to find new and innovative ways of approaching complex issue. Artistic activities greatly enhance the overall learning experience. They promote critical thinking, problem-solving skills, and cognitive development. They foster self-expression, self-confidence, and self-awareness. They promote cultural diversity, social inclusion, and empathy. They enhance mental health and well-being. They improve concentration, focus, and remembering. They promote self-discipline, perseverance, and a growth mindset. And they foster innovation and creativeness. By encouraging and supporting artistic activities, we are not only enhancing individuals' learning experience but also preparing them for achiever in all aspect of their life. Artistic development is not solely a shape of leisure or amusement ; it is a fundamental facet of human growth and development. Creativeness and artistic expression should be encouraged and nurtured at all age, as they have the force to transform individuals and community.

NURTURING A LOVE FOR THE ARTS THROUGH EXPOSURE

As human banners, we have a natural kinship towards creativity and self-expression, and the arts provide us with a unique intermediate to fulfill these need. By exposing individuals to various forms of art, we allow them to explore and discover their own creative abilities. This exposure can take many forms, such as visiting art gallery, attending concert or theatrical performance, or even engaging in hands-on artistic activity like paint or sing. Through these experience, individuals not only gain appreciation for different art forms, but they also unlock their own possible for creativity. Exposure to the arts foster an appreciation for aesthetics and stunner. When individuals are exposed to work of art, they are able to witness the power of artistic manifestation and the stunner that can be conveyed through different medium. This exposure allows individuals to develop a sense of aesthetics, enabling them to appreciate and recognize to valuate of artistic Creation. Whether it is a captivating paint, an emotionally charged slice of euphony, or a powerful dancing execution, exposure to these artistic expression instills a sense of question and reverence in individuals. This appreciation for aesthetics not only enhances one's understanding of the arts but also extends to other aspect of lifetime, such as architecture, designing, and even nature. Exposure to the arts has the power to inspire and spark creativity within individuals. When we witness the imitativeness and invention displayed in artistic work, it triggers our own creative think and encourages us to explore our own artistic abilities. A who attends a concert may be inspired to learn to play a tool or compose their own euphony. Similarly, exposure to painting or sculpture can ignite a love for visual arts and lead individuals to experiment with various artistic technique. By nurturing this love for the arts through exposure, we are providing individuals with the tool and inspiration to tap into their own creative possible. Exposure to the arts promotes cultural understanding and empathy. Art has the power to transcend words and cultural barrier, allowing individuals to connect with others on a deeper tier. By exposing individuals to diverse art forms from around the globe, we broaden their perspective and foster empathy towards different culture and society. This exposure encourages individuals to embrace variety, respect different artistic tradition, and celebrate the magnificence of human manifestation. Through the arts, we can bridge gap between different community and foster a sense of oneness and understanding. Nurturing a love for the arts through exposure is paramount in the development of creativity and artistic skills. By exposing individuals to various art forms, we allow them to appreciate aesthetics, ignite their own creativity, and foster cultural understanding. The arts provide an invaluable intermediate for self-expression and offer a mean for individuals to explore their own creative abilities. Through exposure to the arts, we not only enrich our life with stunner and inspiration but also contribute to the holistic development of individuals and fellowship as a totally. It is essential that we prioritize and promote opportunity for individuals of all ages to engage with the arts, as it is through this exposure that we can fully realize the transformative power of creativity.

FIELD TRIPS TO MUSEUMS, THEATERS, AND GALLERIES

These outing provide students with invaluable opportunity to engage with various forms of art, expanding their artistic horizon and enhancing their creative ability. Museum, Offer a diverse range of art from different period and culture, encouraging students to appreciate and analyze artistic expression across clock and infinite. By exposing students to a superfluity of artistic style and techniques, museum spark their imitativeness and inspire them to experiment with their own artistic Creation. Theater, on the other paw, allow students to experience live performance and witness the transformative force of acting, dancing, and sing. These experience not only expose students to different storytelling techniques, but they also help develop their empathy and emotional news as they engage with the actor' depiction of complex character and narrative. Trips to gallery provide students with the chance to view contemporary art and interact with artists, gaining insight into their creative procedure and the motivation behind their operate. Students can engage in conversation with artists, ask question, and even learn about various art forms through workshop and demonstration. This active encounter with art assist students develop a deep admiration for artistic expression and the diverse range of perspective and idea it encompasses.

GUEST ARTISTS AND PERFORMERS INSPIRING STUDENTS

Another valuable method for encouraging creativity and artistic development in students is through the comprehension of guest artists and performers. By bringing in professionals from various creative fields, students can gain exposure to different styles and techniques that they may not otherwise have access to. These guest artists can serve as mentors and role models, providing guidance and inspiration as students navigate their own artistic journeys. Having professionals visit the campus can expose students to the realities and demands of a career in the arts, helping them to better understand the commitment and dedication required to succeed in this field. One significant gain of guest artists and performers is the chance for students to learn from their expertise and feel. By observing professionals in activity, students can gain insight into the technical skills and artistic techniques that contribute to a successful execution or art. Guest artists can demonstrate different styles or approach, exposing students to diverse perspective and providing them with a broader understanding of their chosen artistic correction. This exposure can be particularly impactful for students who may not have access to such resource in their local community or who are limited by the ambit of their educational program. By bringing in guest artists, colleges and universities give students the opportunity to interact with professionals and learn directly from their expertise, which in turning can help foster the development of students' own artistic skills. Guest artists and performers can also serve as mentors and role models for students, providing guidance, boost, and inspiration. These individual have often gone through similar artistic journeys and can deal their personal experience and advice with students. By hearing about the challenges and successes these professionals have faced, students can gain a feel of view and a better understanding of the possibility that lie ahead in their own artistic pursuit. Having somebody to look up to and learn from can be a powerful incentive, encouraging students to push themselves creatively and strive for excellency in their operate. The connection formed between students and guest artists can continue beyond the initial visit, as students may seek further guidance and mentorship from these professionals even after their clock on campus has ended. In plus to providing mentorship and inspiration, guest artists and performers can also expose students to the realities of a career in the arts. By inviting professionals to visit the campus, colleges and universities can facilitate conversation about the challenges and demands of pursuing a career in the creative industry. This can help students to make informed decision about their artistic next and prepare them for the realities of the professional globe. Understanding the commitment and dedication required for achiever in the arts can be invaluable for students as they navigate their educational and career path. By witnessing the hard operate and love of guest artists and performers, students can develop a realistic understanding of the attempt required to not only excel in their chosen arena but also to find fulfillment and gratification in their creative endeavor. Guest artists and performers play a crucial role in encouraging creativity and the development of artistic skills in college and university students. Through their expertise, mentorship, and exposure to the realities of a career in the arts, students can gain valuable perceptiveness, inspiration, and guidance. By bringing professionals to campus, educational institution provide students with unique and transformative experience that can enhance their artistic journeys and shape their next as creative professionals. Creativity and artistic development are crucial aspect of human growth and should be encouraged at all ages. Artistic expression allows individuals to explore their emotions, communicate their thinking and idea, and gain a deeper understand of themselves and the surrounding globe. From a young age, children possess a natural tendency towards creativity, as evidenced by their passion for drawing, painting, and imaginative run. As they grow older, societal expectation, academic pressures, and a focusing on practicality often stifle their artistic development. It is essential for educators, parents, and society as a totally to recognize the grandness of fostering creativity and providing opportunities for artistic exploration at every phase of life. Encouraging creativity and artistic development in children is of utmost grandness, as it provides them with a powerful vent for self-expression. Through art, children are able to communicate their thinking, feeling, and experience in a path that phrase alone cannot capture. This can be particularly beneficial for children who struggle with verbal communicating or have difficulty expressing their emotions. Artistic activity allow them to externalize their inner globe and deal their unique perspective with others. Engaging in creative endeavor promotes cognitive development, problem-solving skills, and foster a sense of oddity and imitativeness. The meaning of creativity should not be limited to puerility. Adolescence and maturity are equally critical stage for artistic development. During these days, individuals wade through the challenge and transition of self-identity and personal growth. Creativity can serve as a therapeutic and transformative instrument for navigating this complexity. For teen, art can provide them with a sense of bureau and command in to confront of societal and academic pressures. It empowers them to find their vocalization, express their individualism, and embrace their singularity. Artistic activity such as painting, drawing, and writing can serve as cathartic outlet for teenage angst, helping them cope with the emotional up and down that come with adolescence. Similarly, adult can greatly benefit from engaging in creative pursuits. In a globe that often demands accordance and practicality, artistic expression offers a boulevard for self-reflection, personal growth, and renewed delight. It allows adult to reconnect with their inner child, explore new possibility, and challenge their preconceived notion. Creativity promote mental well-being, reduce strain, and enhances overall life gratification. To nurture creativity and artistic development, it is essential to provide individuals with supportive environments that foster artistic exploration at every age. This begins with early education, where art should be an integral component of the syllabus. School should prioritize art class, provide admittance to art supply and material, and encourage student to engage in various artistic medium. Educators should adopt a multidisciplinary overture, integrating art into other subject such as skill, chronicle, and lit. By linking art with academic substance, student are given the chance to develop critical think skills, make connection, and realize complex concept in a more holistic way. Beyond formal education, parents and caregiver play a crucial part in nurturing creativity. They should provide children with opportunities for open-ended run, vulnerability to different form of art, and support their artistic endeavor. This can be achieved by visiting art gallery, museum, and encouraging involvement in community art program. In plus, parents should refrain from imposing predetermined expectation or judgment on their children's artistic expression, allowing them the exemption to explore and experiment without dread of loser. Society should valuate and respect the creative pursuits of individuals at all ages. Artistic endeavor should be encouraged, supported, and celebrated through financing for community art program, public art installation, and recognition of artist' achievements. By fostering an environment that values artistic expression, society can reap the numerous benefit that come with it, including enhanced creativity, invention, and a deeper admiration for the diverse perspective of its member. Creativity and artistic development should be embraced and encouraged at all stage of life. From puerility to adulthood, artistic expression provides individuals with a powerful mean of communicating, personal growth, and self-reflection. Nurturing creativity requires a collaborative attempt from educators, parents, and society, involving the proviso of supportive environments, multidisciplinary education, and recognition of artistic achievements. By fostering creativity and artistic development, we can unlock the full possible of individuals, enrich their life, and create a more vibrant and empathetic society.

VII. ADOLESCENCE

Adolescence, the seventh stage of life according to Erik Erikson's psychosocial hypothesis, is a crucial point for the development of creativity and artistic skills. During this stage, which typically occurs between the age of 12 and 18, individuals experience significant physical, cognitive, and emotional changes. These changes create a unique opportunity for the exploration and expression of artistic abilities. Adolescents often exhibit heightened idealism and a want to discover their own individuality, making it an ideal clock to encourage and nurture their creativity. The increased capability for abstract thinking during this point enables adolescents to think more profoundly about their artistic endeavors and the message they want to convey. The cognitive restructure that takes spot during adolescence allows individuals to engage in more complex problem-solving and decision-making, skills that are essential in artistic discipline. Adolescents can experiment with different artistic technique, material, and style in ordering to develop their own artistic vocalization and flair. The emotional changes that occur during adolescence also contribute to the development of creativity and artistic skills. Adolescents often experience intense emotion and seek outlet for self-expression. Artistic activity provide a mean for individuals to procedure and communicate this emotion in a healthy and constructive way. Whether it is through paint, writing, or perform, adolescents can channel their feeling into their creative operate, allowing them to find publish and self-understanding. Artistic pursuit can foster a sense of belong and community during this stage of life. Adolescents often seek adoption and avowal from their peer, and artistic endeavors can provide a shared concern and generator of comradery. Joining a dramaturgy grouping or participating in a visual humanities' nightspot not only allows adolescents to develop their artistic skills but also offers opportunities for collaboration and social interaction. In this path, artistic development can contribute to the establishment of friendship and the refinement of a supporting web during adolescence. Encouraging creativity and the development of artistic skills in adolescence has long-term benefit. Adolescents who engage in artistic activity are more likely to develop skills such as problem-solving, critical think, and effective communicating - skills that are highly valued in various academic and professional pursuit. The exploration and expression of creativity during this stage can help individuals discover their passion and interest, which can guide their vocation choice and contribute to a sense of fulfillment and aim in life. By encouraging artistic development in adolescence, society not only invests in the personal growth and well-being of individuals but also nurtures the next coevals of artist, innovator, and creative thinkers. Adolescence is a critical stage for the development of creativity and artistic skills. The physical, cognitive, and emotional transformation that occur during this point provide a unique opportunity for individuals to explore and express their artistic abilities. Encourage and supporting artistic development in adolescence not only contributes to personal growth and self-discovery but also cultivates important skills that can benefit individuals in various area of life. By recognizing the meaning of this stage and providing adequate resource and opportunities for artistic exploration, society can foster the growth of future artist and creative thinkers, contributing to a vivacious and culturally rich society.

PROVIDING OPPORTUNITIES FOR SELF-EXPRESSION

Artistic expression allows individuals to explore their feeling, thinking, and idea in a unique and personal path. By providing an infinite for self-expression, individuals can develop a sense of identity and enhance their emotional well-being. This is particularly important for young children, as engaging in creative activities helps them understand and communicate their experience and emotion before they have the verbal skills to do so. The boost of self-expression in young children can foster a positive attitude towards art and creative activities, which can have a lasting impact on their overall artistic development. By providing opportunities for self-expression, individuals are empowered to discover and nurture their unique talent and interest. This can lead to a sense of self-confidence and a greater admiration for the arts. Providing opportunities for self-expression is not limited to young children. Adolescent and adult can also benefit greatly from engaging in creative activities. In now's fast-paced and high-stress globe, many individuals find comfort and loosening through artistic expression. Whether it is painting, writing, playing a musical tool, or dance, engaging in creative activities allows individuals to disconnect from their daily responsibility and express themselves freely. This can have a profound impact on mental health and overall well-being. Inquiry has shown that engaging in creative activities can reduce strain level, improve climate, and even alleviate symptom of anxiousness and slump. By providing opportunities for individuals to explore their creativity and enlist in artistic expression, we can promote mental health and encourage personal increase. Providing opportunities for self-expression encourages collaboration and social interaction. Creative activities such as dramaturgy, euphony ensemble, or studio art workshop often involve working in group or team. These collaborative experience provide individuals with the chance to communicate, deal idea, and learn from others. By engaging in creative collaboration, individuals can develop important skills such as problem-solving, communicating, and teamwork. These skills are not only essential for artistic development but also transferable to other area of lifetime, including the work. By fostering collaboration and social interaction through artistic endeavor, we can nurture well-rounded individuals who are equipped with the skills necessary for achiever in a various and interconnected globe. Providing opportunities for self-expression allows individuals to contribute to their communities and make a positive impact on society. Art has the force to provoke think, gainsay norm, and spark dialog. By encouraging individuals to express themselves artistically, we enable them to deal their unique perspective and contribute to the cultural magnificence of their communities. Whether it is through public art installation, community dramaturgy performance, or literary reading, artistic expression can bring masses together, promote understand, and inspire social alter. By providing opportunities for self-expression, we empower individuals to use their voice and creativity to address important social issue, foster empathy, and create a more inclusive and compassionate society. Providing opportunities for self-expression is crucial for encouraging creativity and the development of artistic skills at all ages. By nurturing self-expression, individuals can develop a sense of identity, enhance their emotional well-being, and foster

a positive attitude towards the arts. Engaging in creative activities promotes mental health, encourages collaboration and social interaction, and allows individuals to contribute to their
communities. As educator, parent, and community member, it is
our obligation to provide space and opportunities for individuals
to explore their creativity and express themselves artistically, as
the benefit extend far beyond the kingdom of art itself.

ARTISTIC OUTLETS AS A MEANS OF EMOTIONAL RELEASE

Artistic outlets, such as paint, writing, or playing a musical tool, have long been recognized as powerful means of emotional release. The act of creating art can provide individuals with a safe and constructive path to channel and express their emotions. Many masses find that engaging in artistic activities allows them to tap into their inner thinking and feeling, helping them to better understand and process complex emotions. This can be particularly beneficial for individuals who struggle with verbal expression, as art provides an alternative method of communication. Through art, individuals are able to create visual representation of their emotions, allowing them to externalize and confront their inner upheaval. By using color, shape, and line, artist can convey their emotions with a tier of deepness and subtlety that phrase often fail to seize. The process of creating art itself can serve as a shape of therapy, enabling individuals to find comfort and solace in the act of innovation. For many individuals, engaging in artistic activities provides a sense of catharsis. The act of creating art allows individuals to release pent-up emotions and experiences, providing a sense of relief and release. This is particularly true in instance where emotions are too overwhelming or complex to be articulated through traditional means of communication. Through art, individuals can explore and express the full array of their emotions, including those that are difficult or verboten. This process of emotional release can have a transformative consequence, enabling individuals to gain a greater sense of clearness and understanding of their own emotional landscape. Engaging in artistic outlets can provide a sense of authorization and control over one's own emotions. Creating art allows individuals to take bureau over their emotions, transforming them into something tangible and manageable. In this path, art becomes an instrument for self-expression and self-discovery, allowing individuals to navigate and make sense of their own emotional journey. By externalizing and confronting their emotions through art, individuals gain a sense of domination and control over their own experiences, enhancing their overall sense of well-being. Artistic outlets also have the ability to foster connection and facilitate emotional healing. Through creative expression, individuals are able to connect with others on a deep and personal tier, fostering a sense of empathy and understanding. Art form, such as dramaturgy or euphony, have the force to elicit emotional response in both the Almighty and the interview, creating a shared experience that promotes connection and healing. Engaging in artistic activities within a supportive community can provide individuals with a sense of belong and validation. Artistic community often serve as safe space where individuals can openly express themselves without dread of opinion or rejection. Within this community, individuals can form relationship with others who deal their experiences and emotions, finding supporting and validation in their artistic endeavor. Artistic outlets provide individuals with a means of emotional release and self-expression. Through art, individuals are able to externalize and confront complex emotions, providing a sense of relief and catharsis. Engaging in artistic activities also empowers individuals to take control of their emotions and gain a deeper understanding of their emotional landscape. Art has the ability to foster connection and facilitate emotional healing by providing individuals with an intermediate to express themselves and connect with others. Thus, encouraging the developing of artistic skill and promoting creativeness at all age is crucial in supporting individuals in their emotional well-being and personal increase.

ARTISTIC COMMUNITIES FOSTERING A SENSE OF BELONGING

Being part of an artistic community provides individuals with a sense of adoption and understand that may be lacking in other aspect of their life. In these communities, individuals can express themselves freely without fear of opinion or critique. They are surrounded by like-minded individuals who share similar passion and interest, creating an environment where their love for art is not only appreciated but celebrated. This sense of belonging can be especially vital for individuals who may feel marginalized or misunderstand in mainstream society. Individuals who identify as LGBTQ+ may find comfort and adoption within artistic communities that are known for their inclusivity and festivity of variety. Individuals from different cultural background can come together in artistic communities to learn from and appreciate each other's art form, promoting cross-cultural understand and unity. These communities also provide a support scheme for individuals, nurturing their artistic growth and development. Artist within these communities often collaborate and inspire each other, pushing one another to reach new creative pinnacle. The feedback and direction received from fellow artist can be invaluable in helping individuals refine their skills and explore new artistic avenue. The sense of comradery and mutual support within artistic communities can help individuals overcome challenge and setback that are inherent to the creative procedure. Artistic communities provide a safe infinite where individuals can experiment, take risk, and learn from their mistake without fear of loser. This supportive environment encourage individuals to explore their creativity and develop their artistic skills to their fullest possible. The sense of belonging fostered within these communities extends beyond the artistic kingdom and can have a positive effect on individuals' overall well-being. Inquiry has shown that belongingness is a fundamental psychological want, and fulfilling this want contributes to higher level of felicity and lifetime gratification. When individuals feel a sense of belonging, they are more likely to have positive mental wellness outcome, such as reduced feelings of aloneness, anxiousness, and slump. Artistic communities offer individuals the opportunity to connect with others who share their interest and passion, reducing feelings of isolation and providing a sense of aim and fulfillment. Being part of an artistic community can also enhance individuals' social skills and interpersonal relationships. Through collaborative project, grouping exhibition, and workshop, individuals learn how to effectively communicate, cooperate, and negotiate with others. These skills are not only valuable within the artistic community but also transferable to other area of their life, such as the work and personal relationships. Artistic communities play a vital role in fostering a sense of belonging among individuals. They create a supportive environment where individuals feel valued, understand, and accepted for their love of art. This sense of belonging not only nurtures individuals' artistic growth and development but also contributes to their overall well-being and felicity. Whether it is through collaboration, aspiration, or simply the opportunity to connect with like-minded individuals, artistic communities provide a unique infinite for individuals to explore their creativity and develop their artistic skills. By fostering a sense

of belonging, these communities empower individuals to express
themselves authentically and contribute to the rich tapes of artistic manifestation in our society.

DEVELOPING CRITICAL THINKING AND CREATIVITY

Critical thinking involves the power to analyze information and make well-informed decisions. It is a crucial skill in various aspects of lifetime, including education, vocation, and problem-solving. By nurturing critical thinking, individuals can develop a deeper understand of complex topic, enhance their cognitive abilities, and make sound judgment. Creativity is equally important as it allows individuals to explore different perspectives, generate innovative ideas, and find unique solutions to problem. Whether in the arts or sciences, creativity plays a vital part in pushing boundary, challenging conventional thinking, and driving progression. In the kingdom of education, the refinement of critical thinking and creativity is crucial to fostering an engage and stimulating learning surroundings. When student are encouraged to think critically, they are able to question the information they are presented with and delve deeper into subject. This promotes active learn and helps student develop problem-solving skills. As student engage in critical thinking, they become more independent and confident learner, capable of analyzing information from multiple perspectives. By integrating creativity into the educational procedure, educator can enable student to think outside the box and overture problem with innovative solutions. This in turning prepare them for the challenge they will face in their next career. Critical thinking and creativity are fundamental to achiever in the modern manpower. In now's dynamic and rapidly changing globe, employer are increasingly seeking individuals who can think critically and adapt to new situation. Critical thinking allows employees to evaluate information objectively, assess risk, and make informed decisions. It also enables them to identify potential problem and develop effective solutions. In plus, creativity is highly valued in the work as it drives invention and foster a competitive boundary. Creativity allows employees to approach task with a fresh perspective, leading to new and innovative ideas that can propel a clientele ahead. Thus, individuals who possess strong critical thinking and creativity skills are more likely to thrive in their career and contribute to the increase and achiever of their organization. Critical thinking and creativity are not limited to specific discipline or fields of survey ; they are essential for any intellectual chase. In the arts, critical thinking helps individuals analyze and interpret work of art, fostering a deeper admiration and understand. Creativity, on the other hand, allows artist to experiment with different technique and style, leading to the innovation of unique and captivating artwork. In the sciences, critical thinking enables researcher to question existing theory, devise hypothesis, and designing experiment. Creativity in the sciences often leads to breakthroughs and advancement in various fields. Integrating critical thinking and creativity into both the arts and sciences enhances the overall caliber and affect of intellectual endeavor. Developing critical thinking and creativity is crucial for individuals of all age and in various domains. Whether in education, the manpower, or intellectual pursuit, critical thinking allows individuals to analyze information, make informed decisions, and develop problem-solving skills. Creativity, on the other hand, encourages individuals to think outside the box, generate innovative ideas, and find unique solutions.

By cultivating these skills, individuals can enhance their cognitive abilities, broaden their perspectives, and contribute to progression and increase in their respective fields.

ENCOURAGING EXPERIMENTATION AND RISK-TAKING IN ART

Artistic development is a liquid and ever-evolving process that requires the boost of experimentation and risk-taking. When individual are given the freedom to explore different mediums, techniques, and ideas, they are more likely to discover unique perspectives and push the boundaries of their creativity. By fostering an environment that promotes experimentation, artists are able to develop their skills and create meaningful and innovative work of art. Allowing for experimentation in art allows artists to break free from conventional norm and explore new possibilities. When artists are encouraged to go beyond their comfort zones and try new thing, they are able to explore different style and techniques that they may not have otherwise considered. This process of experimentation can lead to the development of their own unique artistic voice and style. By taking risks and stepping outside their comfort zones, artists are able to challenge themselves and push the boundaries of their own artistic abilities. Experimentation also opens up opportunity for learning and increase. By trying new techniques or mediums, artists are able to expand their skill set and develop a deeper understanding of their craftsmanship. They can gain new perspectives and insight that can further enhance their artistic abilities. Through experimentation, artists can learn from both their successes and failure, allowing them to develop their skills and strengthen their artistic exercise. Encouraging experimentation and risk-taking in art fosters a civilization of invention and creativity. When artists are given the freedom to explore and take risks, they are more likely to come up with unique and ground-breaking ideas. The creative process thrive on experimentation and the exploration of new possibilities. By encouraging artists to take risks, we are opening up the possible for groundbreaking artistic creations that may have never been imagined before. In plus, experimentation and risk-taking in art can lead to personal and self-exploration. Art has the force to connect individual with their inner selves and provide a mean for self-expression. When artists are encouraged to experiment and take risks, they are able to delve deeper into their own emotion, thinking, and experience. This process of self-exploration can be incredibly transformative, allowing artists to gain a greater understanding of themselves and their spot in the globe. Embracing experimentation and risk-taking in art fosters a feel of resilience and adaptability. Artistic development is often marked by up and down, successes and failure. By encouraging artists to take risks and experiment, we are teaching them to embrace loser as a learn chance and to persist in to confront of hardship. This resilience and adaptability are not only valuable in the artistic globe but also in other aspect of lifetime. Artists who have learned to take risks and experiment are better equipped to navigate challenge and find creative solution. Encouraging experimentation and risk-taking in art is essential for the development of artists at all level. By allowing artists to explore different mediums, techniques, and ideas, we provide them with the freedom to discover their own unique artistic voice and style. Experimentation fosters personal increase, invention, and self-exploration, while also cultivating resilience and adaptability. As we foster an environment that embraces experimentation,

we can expect to see the growth of groundbreaking artistic creations that push the boundaries of creativity and inspire new
possibilities.

ARTISTIC PURSUITS AS A WAY TO EXPLORE PERSONAL IDENTITY

Artistic pursuits offer a unique and valuable avenue for individuals to explore and understand their personal identity. By engaging in various art forms and creative activities, individuals are able to delve into their emotion, thoughts, and experiences, facilitating a deeper understanding of who they are as individuals. Artistic manifestation enables individuals to communicate their innermost thoughts and feeling in a way that is often difficult to achieve through other medium. Whether it is through paint, writing, dancing, or any other artistic form, the creative process allows individuals to explore and express their own unique perspectives and experiences. One way in which artistic pursuits can aid in the exploration of personal identity is by providing an intermediate through which individuals can document and reflect upon their life experiences. Art allows individuals to capture their thoughts and emotion at specific moment in clock, creating a tangible theatrical of their identity at that particular crossroads. A lens man may choose to capture a series of image that symbolize their journeying of self-discovery, allowing them to reflect on how their experiences have shaped their identity. Similarly, an author may use verse or prose as a mean of exploring and expressing their personal increase and developing over clock. Art offers a safe infinite for individuals to experiment with different perspectives and identities. Through artistic pursuits, individuals have the chance to step outside their usual role and explore alternative narrative and possibility.

This can be particularly valuable for individuals who are grappling with question of self-identity or experiencing a point of changeover in their lives. A choreographer may use dancing as a way to explore different aspects of their personality, trying on different movement and style to better understand who they are as a Terpsichore and as an individual. By experimenting with new forms of artistic manifestation, individuals may discover previously unknown aspects of themselves, leading to a greater understanding and adoption of their personal identity. Engaging in artistic pursuits allows individuals to confront and challenge societal expectations and norms, providing a program for the exploration of personal value and belief. Art has the force to challenge deeply ingrained idea and stereotype, allowing individuals to express their true self in a way that may not be possible in their everyday lives. A visual artist may choose to create a series of abstract painting that challenge societal notion of stunner or query traditional sexuality role. Through the process of creating and sharing this artwork, individuals are able to assert their own unique perspectives and value, contributing to the ongoing dialog around personal identity and societal expectations. Artistic pursuits offer a valuable avenue for individuals to explore and understand their personal identity. By engaging in various art forms and creative activities, individuals are able to document and reflect upon their life experiences, experiment with different perspectives and identities, and challenge societal expectations and norms. The creative process enables individuals to communicate their innermost thoughts and feeling, facilitating a deeper understanding of who they are as individuals. As such, it is crucial to encourage and support artistic developing at all age, as it not only promotes self-expression and self-discovery, but also contributes to the broader cultural and societal discussion surrounding personal identity. Beyond the misconception that creativity and artistic development are pursuit reserved for a select few individuals with inborn endowment, lies the realism that creativity and artistic skills can be nurtured and developed at all age. In fact, it is crucial to encourage creativity and artistic development throughout all stage of life, as doing so can bring about numerous benefit and enhance one's overall well-being. From childhood to adulthood and old age, fostering creativity and honing artistic skills can promote cognitive development, emotional expression, and personal growth. It is important to acknowledge that creativity manifests itself in various forms, and nurturing creativity means recognizing and fostering diverse artistic endeavors, be it in painting, writing, music, or dancing. During childhood, creativity and artistic development play a fundamental part in cognitive growth. Through various creative activities, such as draw, painting, and construction, child engage in critical think and problem-solving, enabling them to gain a deep understand of the surrounding globe. Creative endeavors help them develop their visual-spatial skills and enhance their power to perceive and interpret the surroundings. By encouraging child to experiment with different material and engage in imaginative task, parent and educator can foster their creativity and promote tractability and adaptability in their think. As individuals changeover into adolescence and young adulthood, creativity and artistic development continue to be essential for personal growth and self-expression. Adolescent often face individuality establishment challenge, as they explore different aspect of their personality and sail through societal pressure. Engaging in artistic pursuit provides them with a means of self-expression and allows them to discover and develop their individualism. Whether it be through writing, photography, or music, artistic outlet offer a program for adolescent to express their thinking, emotion, and experience. This not only enhances their communicating skills but also fosters a sense of self-worth and trust, promoting positive mental wellness outcome. Artistic development during adulthood can serve as a means of personal fulfillment and strain succor. As individuals juggle operate and personal responsibility, engaging in creative activities provides a vent for loosening and introspection. Whether it be through painting, playing a musical tool, or engaging in writing, adults can immerse themselves in their creative pursuit and find comfort in the procedure. The act of creating allow adults to temporarily detach from everyday stressor and enter a commonwealth of flowing, where they can focus on the present minute and achieve a sense of achievement. Pursuing artistic endeavors can expand one's social encircle and provide opportunity for collaboration and community participation, further enhancing personal well-being. Creativity and artistic development are not limited to any specific age or phase of life, as they continue to be important in old age. In fact, engaging in creative activities can have numerous positive effect on older adults' cognitive ability and emotional well-being. Study have shown that participating in artistic endeavors, such as painting or sculpt, can improve cognitive function such as remembering, care, and problem-solving skills. Engaging in artistic activities provides older adults with a sense of aim, promoting their mental and emotional well-being. Whether it be through joining art class or participating in community art event, older adults can continue to develop their artistic skills and enjoy the benefit of creativity well into their golden days. Fostering creativity and artistic development at all age is essential for cognitive development, emotional expression, and personal growth. From childhood to adulthood and old age, engaging in creative activities enhances cognitive skills, promotes self-expression, and contributes to overall well-being. It is crucial to recognize and support diverse artistic endeavors and provide individuals with opportunity to explore and develop their creativity. By doing so, we will not only enrich our life but also create a fellowship that celebrates and value artistic expression.

VIII. ADULTHOOD

Adulthood marks a stage in lifetime where individuals are expected to assume greater responsibility and independence. It is a point characterized by significant shift in various domains, including personal growth, career development, and relationship. Despite the demand and challenge that come with adulthood, it is crucial to recognize and nurture creativity and artistic development in individuals during this stage. Many masses tend to believe that creativity is limited to puerility and adolescence, often associating it with ingenuousness and a deficiency of inhibition. To dismiss the importance of creativity in adulthood would be a grave error. One of the primary reason why creativity and artistic development should be encouraged in adulthood is because it fosters personal growth and self-expression. As individuals changeover into adulthood, they often experience increased self-awareness and a want to redefine their identity. Exploring various creative outlets, such as paint, writing, or euphony, can provide a mean of process and expressing complex emotion and thinking. To behave of creating something tangible allows individuals to connect with their inner self and communicate their ideas and perspectives in a unique and individualistic way. Through creativity, adults can tap into their imagination, explore new possibility, and deepen their understanding of themselves and the world around them. Encouraging creativity and artistic development in adulthood can have profound effect on one's mental health and overall well-being. The demand of adulthood, whether related to career, kinfolk, or personal goal, can often be overwhelming and stressful. Engaging in creative pursuits can serve as a shape of self-care, promoting relaxation, strain decrease, and improved mental clearness. The procedure of creating art can provide a sense of flowing and mindfulness, allowing individuals to immerse themselves in the present minute and find solace from the pressure of daily lifetime. Inquiry has consistently shown a correlation between participation in artistic activity and positive mental health outcome, including increased self-esteem, enhanced climate, and reduced symptom of anxiousness and slump. By prioritizing creativity in adulthood, individuals can cultivate a greater sense of well-being and equilibrium in their lives. In plus to the personal benefit, fostering creativity and artistic development in adulthood also has social significance. Art has the force to bridge divide, spur conversation, and create connection between individuals from different background and perspectives. Engaging in artistic endeavor can provide opportunity for network, collaboration, and community construction. Whether through involvement in art class, attending gallery and exhibition, or joining community art group, adults can form meaningful relationship with like-minded individuals who deal a common love for creativity. This connection not only enrich their social lives but also expose them to new ideas and perspectives, encouraging personal growth and expanding their understanding of the world. Creativity in adulthood can contribute to career development and professional success. In now's rapidly changing and dynamic task marketplace, creativity is increasingly valued by employer across various industry. Creative problem-solving skill, innovative think, and out-of-the-box ideas have become essential assets in the corporate world. By nurturing creativity and artistic development in adulthood, individuals can enhance their power to adapt to new challenge, engender unique solution, and stance themselves as valuable assets in their professional endeavor. Engaging in creative pursuits outside operate can provide individuals with a sense of fulfillment and love that can positively impact their overall task gratification and work-life equilibrium. Adulthood is a stage of lifetime that should not exclude the importance of creativity and artistic development. Encouraging creative manifestation in adulthood fosters personal growth, supports mental health, facilitates social connection, and contributes to professional success. Adults who embrace their creativity and enlist in artistic pursuits can tap into their inner self, find solace and relaxation, connect with others, and enhance their problem-solving ability. By recognizing and nurturing creativity in adulthood, we can unlock the transformative force of art and enable individuals to fully embrace the possible of this stage in their lives.

ENCOURAGING LIFELONG LEARNING AND PERSONAL GROWTH

Encouraging lifelong learning and personal growth is crucial for individuals to broaden their horizon and achieve their full potential. Lifelong learning entail adopting a continuous attitude of curiosity and seeking knowledge, not only through formal teaching but also through informal experience and personal exploration. This mentality allows individuals to continually enhance their skills and stay updated with the latest developments in their fields of concern. Lifelong learning cultivates a sense of self-motivation and authorization as individuals take command of their own personal growth and seize opportunities for development. Participating in lifelong learning activities promotes personal growth by fostering intellectual stimulation, critical thinking, and problem-solving skills. By engaging in activities such as read, attending workshop or seminar, and participating in discussion, individuals are challenged to consider different perspectives, think critically about complex issue, and come up with innovative solution. These skills are not only vital for personal growth but also for professional achiever in now's rapidly evolving globe. They enable individuals to adapt to changing circumstance and prosper in an assortment of context. Lifelong learning also encourages personal growth by fostering creativity and fostering a spirit of innovation. By exploring different fields, individuals gain vulnerability to diverse ideas, perspectives, and methodologies. This vulnerability, combined with the cognitive nimbleness developed through continuous learning, allows individuals to think creatively and approach problem from unique angle. By embracing the mentality of lifelong learning, individuals can break free from traditional mode of thinking and discover new opportunities for personal growth and development. Encouraging lifelong learning and personal growth has a positive impact on individuals' mental health and overall well-being. Engaging in intellectual pursuit and challenging oneself with new knowledge and experience can promote a sense of purpose, fulfillment, and self-actualization. Lifelong learning can serve as a powerful instrument for personal reflection, self-discovery, and personal fulfillment. It provides individuals with the chance to explore their passions, discover new interest, and pursue meaningful goal. By continuously learning, individuals are more likely to lead purposeful lives that align with their values, strength, and aspirations. This sense of purpose and fulfillment can contribute to improved mental health, increased resiliency, and better overall well-being. Encouraging lifelong learning and personal growth is crucial for individuals to achieve their full potential, broaden their horizon, and enhance their overall well-being. By adopting a continuous attitude of curiosity and seeking knowledge, individuals can engage in activities that promote intellectual stimulation, critical thinking, and problem-solving skills. Lifelong learning foster creativity and a spirit of innovation by exposing individuals to diverse ideas, perspectives, and methodologies. Engaging in lifelong learning can have a positive impact on individuals' mental health and overall well-being, as it promotes personal reflection, self-discovery, and fulfillment. By actively participating in lifelong learning activities, individuals can enhance their skills, stay updated with the latest developments in their fields, and lead purposeful lives that align with their values and aspirations. It is essential to promote lifelong learning and personal growth in ordering to empower individuals to become lifelong learner, pursue their passions, and reach their full potential.

ARTISTIC HOBBIES AS A SOURCE OF FULFILLMENT AND RELAXATION

Artistic hobbies can be a prominent source of fulfillment and loosening, offering individuals a unique opportunity to express themselves and explore their creativity. Engaging in artistic activities, such as paint, sculpting, or writing, can nurture a sense of accomplishment and gratification as individuals witness their vision come to life. When masses immerse themselves in these activities, they find solace and reprieve from the stress of daily life, entering a state of flowing where clock seems to disappear, and they become fully absorbed in the creative procedure. One significant facet of artistic hobbies is that they allow individuals to freely express their emotions and thoughts. Through art, masses can communicate their inmost feeling, desire, and experience, often transcending the limitation of verbal words. This shape of manifestation can be immensely therapeutic, providing individuals a vent for their emotions and a mean to process their complexity. Particularly, in case where individuals struggle to articulate their emotions, engaging in artistic hobbies becomes crucial for their mental well-being. The act of creating something visual or conceptual out of one's emotions can bring a sense of clearness and publish, ultimately contributing to personal fulfillment. Artistic hobbies offer a break from the quotidian routine of everyday life. Many individuals find themselves caught up in the fast-paced nature of modern fellowship, constantly juggling responsibility and commitment. Engaging in artistic activities allows masses to step back from their hectic life

and immerse themselves in a globe of creativity and imitativeness. Artist often reports losing racetrack of clock while engaged
in their craftsmanship, which can be a refreshing break from the
demand of operate or schooling. For some, this state of flowing
can even be described as contemplative, providing an opportunity for deep loosening and greening. Artistic hobbies also foster a sense of achievement and personal growth. As individuals
hone their artistic skills, they witness their progression over
clock, which can be immensely gratifying. This sense of accomplishment motivate individuals to continue pursuing their artistic
endeavors, continuously pushing themselves to refine their skills
and experimentation with new technique. Exploring various artistic medium and style can broaden an individual's view and
enhance their creative think ability. The procedure of problem-
solving and the want to think outside the corner when faced
with artistic challenge nurtures a growth mentality and foster
personal developing. Artistic hobbies have the force to connect
individuals with their communities. Art has the ability to transcend cultural and linguistic barrier, making it a universal word
that can be understood and appreciated by masses from different background. Participating in local art exhibit or joining community art group provides an opportunity for individuals to deal
their Creation with others, fostering a sense of belong and comradery. By showcasing their art, individuals not only gain acknowledgment and substantiation for their creative effort but
also contribute to the cultural enrichment of their communities.
Artistic hobbies offer individuals a significant source of fulfillment and loosening. The ability to freely express emotions and
thoughts, to elude from everyday routine, the sense of achievement and personal growth, and the opportunity to connect with

communities all contribute to the immense valuate of engaging in artistic endeavors. By nurturing creativity and the developing of artistic skills, individuals can experience the many benefits that these hobbies offer, contributing to their overall well-being and enriching their life with mean and aim.

CONTINUING EDUCATION IN THE ARTS FOR PERSONAL DEVELOPMENT

Continuing education in the arts is essential for personal developing, as it allows individuals to explore their creativity and further develop their artistic skills throughout their lives. While formal education in the arts is typically focused on a specific point of clock, continuing education provides an opportunity for individuals to continue to learn and grow in their artistic pursuit. Whether it is through attending workshops, taking classes, or participating in art programs, individuals can gain new perspectives, refine their techniques, and expand their artistic horizons. One of the primary benefit of continuing education in the arts is the opportunity to explore one's creativity. As individuals progress through their educational journeying and lifetime experience, it is natural for their creative instinct to evolve and change. Engaging in continuing education allows individuals to tap into their current commonwealth of creativity and explore new way of expressing themselves. By exploring different artistic mediums, techniques, and styles, individuals can find new avenue for self-expression and develop their own unique artistic vocalization. Continuing education in the arts enables individuals to refine their artistic skills. Just like any other skill, artistic abilities require exercise and subtlety to grow. By participating in workshops, classes, or other educational programs, individuals can receive valuable feedback from instructor and fellow artist. This feedback can help them identify area for betterment, overcome challenge, and refine their techniques. Engaging in this educational experience can expose individuals to new approaches, perspectives, and idea that they may not have encountered otherwise. This exposure can challenge individuals to think outside their solace zone and push the boundary of their artistic abilities. In addition to exploring creativity and refine skills, continuing education in the arts offers individuals the opportunity to expand their artistic horizons. The arts have always been interconnected, with different mediums and artistic styles influencing and inspiring one another. By engaging in continuing education, individuals can gain exposure to different art form, styles, and culture. This exposure can broaden their artistic perspective, inspire new idea, and provide fresh source of aspiration. A cat amount may take a sculpt class to learn about three-dimensional shape and how it can inform their two-dimensional work. Similarly, an instrumentalist may take a photography class to explore visual storytelling and incorporate it into their composition. The possibility for interdisciplinary exploration and collaboration are endless in continuing education in the arts. Continuing education in the arts can provide personal fulfillment and enrichment. The arts have the force to evoke emotion, gainsay perception, and connect masses with themselves and others on a deep tier. By engaging in continuing education, individuals can cultivate a lifelong love and admiration for the arts. This can bring a sense of aim and mean to one's lifetime, providing a vent for personal manifestation and exploration. Continuing education in the arts can foster a sense of community and belong among like-minded individuals. The shared experience and discussion that occur in workshops and classes can create meaningful connection and invigorate individuals to continue to learn and grow together. Continuing education in the arts is essential for personal developing as it allows individuals to explore their creativity, refine their artistic skills, expand their artistic horizons, and find personal fulfillment and enrichment. By engaging in workshops, classes, and other educational programs, individuals can continually learn and grow in their artistic pursuit throughout their lives. Whether it is through exploring new mediums, refining techniques, or embracing interdisciplinary approaches, continuing education provides endless opportunity for personal and artistic developing.

PROMOTING CREATIVITY IN PROFESSIONAL SETTINGS

Promoting creativity in professional settings is crucial for fostering innovation, productiveness, and employee gratification. In today's rapidly changing globe, organizations are constantly seeking new and innovative way to meet the evolving need of their customer. As such, creativity has become a highly desirable accomplishment in the professional kingdom. The publicity of creativity in professional settings is not always easy to achieve. Many organizations are inherently risk-averse and prioritize efficiency and predictability over experiment and innovation. Nevertheless, there are several strategies that can be employed to encourage and cultivate creativity in the workplace. One path to promote creativity in professional settings is by creating a supportive and inclusive work environment. Employees need to feel safe and empowered to express their ideas and take risk. This can be achieved by fostering a culture of confidence, where open and transparent communicating is encouraged. Leadership should actively listen to their employees, provide constructive feedback, and valuate various perspectives. In plus, a feel of psychological safe should be instilled, allowing employees to feel comfortable voicing their thinking without dread of opinion or vengeance. When employees feel valued and their ideas are respected, they are more likely to think creatively and contribute to the organization's innovation effort. Another important component in promoting creativity is providing employees with the resource and tool they need to unleash their creative potential.

This includes admittance to relevant technology, training program, and developing opportunity. Organizations should invest in continuous learn and provide employees with the necessary skill and knowledge to think creatively and adapt to changing circumstance. They should create space that facilitate collaboration and brainstorm. Collaborative work environment can foster creativity by allowing employees to bounce ideas off each other, sparking new insight and perspectives. It is essential to promote a healthy work-life balance to enhance employees' creativity and well-being. Overworking and burnout can stifle creativity, as individual are less likely to think creatively when they are stressed and exhausted. Organizations should encourage employees to take break, engage in recreational activity, and pursue hobby outside of work. Incorporating element of run and merriment into the workplace can stimulate creativity. Providing opportunity for employees to engage in activity such as team-building exercise, workshop, or creative challenge can foster a positive and imaginative work environment. Organizations can promote creativity by embracing diversity and inclusivity. Inquiry has shown that diverse team are more innovative and able to generate more creative ideas. By fostering a diverse manpower, organizations can admittance a wider array of perspectives, experience, and knowledge, which can lead to more creative problem-solving. It is important to create an environment where individual from different background and with different identity feel welcome and valued. Promoting diversity at all level of the organization, from enlisting to leaders position, can help nurture a culture of creativity and foster innovation. Promoting creativity in professional settings is crucial for organizations that want to thrive in today's dynamic and competitive globe. Creating a supportive and inclusive work environment, providing employees with the necessary resource, promoting work-life balance, and embracing diversity are all essential strategy to foster creativity in the workplace. When employees are empowered and encouraged to think outside the corner, organizations are more likely to generate innovative ideas and remain relevant in their industry. By prioritizing creativity, organizations can unlock their employees' full creative potential and drive increase and achiever.

BENEFITS OF CREATIVITY IN PROBLEM-SOLVING AND INNOVATION

Creativity plays a vital part in problem-solving and innovation, bringing forward a throng of benefits. Firstly, creativity allows individuals to think outside the corner and explore unconventional solutions to problem. When faced with a complex topic, individuals who embrace creativity are more likely to come up with unique and innovative approach, rather than relying on traditional method. This ability to think beyond established boundary opens up new avenue for problem-solving, leading to more effective and efficient solutions. Creativity fosters a sense of tractability and adaptability in individuals, enabling them to pivot and adjust their strategy when faced with unexpected challenge. Rather than being resistant to change, creative individuals are more open to exploring new possibility and adapting their ideas, allowing for continuous betterment and innovation. Creativity contribute to the developing of critical thinking skill, enhancing the ability to analyze and evaluate different option. When confronted with a problem, creative individuals are equipped with the tool to assess various perspectives, considering not only the immediate solution but also the long-term significance and consequence. This critical thinking mentality encourages a comprehensive valuation of all available choice, leading to more informed decision-making. Creativity encourages individuals to approach problem from multiple angle, promoting a more holistic understand of the position. By considering various viewpoint and incorporating diverse perspectives, creative problem-solving becomes more inclusive and effective.

Creativity fosters an surrounding of collaboration and team-work, facilitating the interchange of ideas and the coevals of innovative solutions. In problem-solving process, bringing together individuals with various background and skillets often leads to a broad array of perspectives and a more comprehensive approach. When creativity is encouraged, individuals feel empowered to contribute their ideas, creating a collaborative ambience that nurtures innovation. By embracing creativity, individuals are more likely to engage in brainstorm session, allowing for the cross-pollination of thinking and the exploration of unfamiliar territory. This collaborative problem-solving approach benefits from the variety of ideas, leading to breakthrough innovation that would not have been possible without the donation of multiple perspectives. Creativity in problem-solving and innovation encourages individuals to take risk and embrace incertitude. Often, dread of loser or the unknown hinder individuals from exploring new possibility. Creativity instills a sense of courage, encouraging individuals to adventure into uncharted territory and experimentation with novel ideas. By embracing the incertitude that comes with creativity, individuals unlock their potential for innovation, discovering novel approach and solutions that may have been overlooked through conventional mean. The feel gained from overcoming challenge and taking risk in a creative problem-solving procedure fosters resiliency and adaptability, character that are invaluable in now's ever-changing globe. Creativity is a driving coerce behind problem-solving and innovation, offering numerous benefits. From promoting out-of-the-box thinking to fostering collaboration and encouraging risk-taking, creativity strengthens problem-

solving capability and paves the way for groundbreaking innovation. Embracing creativity allows individuals to approach
challenge with a fresh perspective, leading to more effective and
efficient solutions. The critical thinking skill developed through
creativity enable individuals to analyze and evaluate option in
a comprehensive and informed way. By championing creativity,
we not only unlock our individual possible but also pave the way
for a more innovative and progressive fellowship.

ARTISTIC SKILLS AS A VALUABLE ASSET IN VARIOUS CAREERS

Artistic skills are often undervalued in various career, as they are often seen as an opulence rather than a necessary. It is crucial to recognize the true valuate that artistic skills bring to a wide array of professions. Whether it is in the field of business, technology, or healthcare, individuals with artistic skills offer a unique perspective and a set of abilities that can greatly enhance their effectiveness in their respective fields. In the world of business, artistic skills can be a valuable plus in creating compelling merchandising material and advertisement. With the rising of digital medium, company are increasingly relying on visually appealing substance to capture the care of their objective interview. Artists with a keen eyeball for designing can play a pivotal part in developing engaging visuals that effectively communicate a party's content. Artistic skills can also contribute to the development of brand mark identity, as professional with an understanding of coloration hypothesis and makeup can create logo, package, and other visual element that accurately represent a brandmark's value and personality. In the kingdom of technology, artistic skills are highly sought after for user feel (UX) and user port (UI) designing. Good UX and UI designing are crucial for creating intuitive and visually appealing digital product. Artists who have a deep understanding of how to visually communicate idea can greatly contribute to the development of user-friendly interface and engaging user experience. By applying their artistic skills, these individuals can create visually appealing interface that are not only aesthetically pleasing but also enhance serviceability and functionality. Further, artistic skills are invaluable in healthcare professions. Art therapy, Utilizes artistic expression as a mean to promote heal and improved mental well-being. Artistic skills allow therapist to facilitate self-discovery and emotional expression in their patient, helping them procedure injury, reduce anxiousness, and enhance their overall caliber of lifetime. Healthcare professional such as surgeon and dentist can benefit from artistic skills, as preciseness and sleight are essential in performing intricate procedure. Artists possess these skills naturally, making them well-equipped to excel in these demanding professions. Artistic skills are not limited to specific industry but can also be applied in various other domains. Architect rely heavily on artistic skills to create visually stunning and functional structure. The ability to visualize and conceptualize three-dimensional space is a crucial facet of their operate. Artists, with their inherent bent for perspective and ratio, bring a unique perspective to the board, resulting in innovative and aesthetically pleasing architectural design. Artistic skills can also be valuable in the field of teaching. Teacher who incorporate art into their syllabus can stimulate creativity and enlist student in a unique and meaningful path. By encouraging artistic expression, educator foster critical think, problem-solving, and self-confidence in their student. Artistic skills also enable teacher to design visually appealing learning material that enhance inclusion and make learning more enjoyable. Artistic skills can also contribute to invention and problem-solving. Artists possess the ability to think outside the corner, approaching challenge from unconventional angle. Their creative think can lead to innovative solution, pushing the boundary of what is possible. Whether it is finding novel way to approach merchandising strategy, developing groundbreaking technology, or designing unique healthcare treatment, individuals with artistic skills have the potential to make a significant effect on the world around them. Artistic skills are highly valuable in a wide range of career. From business and technology to healthcare and teaching, individuals with artistic skills offer a unique perspective and a set of abilities that can greatly enhance their effectiveness in their respective fields. It is essential to recognize and appreciate the true valuate of artistic skills, and to foster creativity and the development of artistic abilities at all age. One of the most important aspect of creativity and artistic development is that it should be encouraged at all age. Whether one is a young child or an adult, fostering creativity and the development of artistic skills can have numerous benefits. For young children, encouraging creativity allows them to express themselves and think outside the corner. This helps them develop problem-solving skills, as well as the power to think critically and imaginatively. By engaging in artistic activities such as draw, painting, and sculpt, children learn to explore their environs and develop a sense of oddity about the world around them. They also learn how to communicate their thinking and emotions through visual means, which can help them develop important social and emotional skills. A child who loves to draw may create art that reflects their feeling and experience, allowing them to express themselves in a way that phrase cannot. This can be especially beneficial for children who may struggle with verbal communicating or have difficulty expressing their emotions. Creativity and artistic development should not be restricted to just children, but should be encouraged and nurtured throughout one's lifetime. For adults, engaging in artistic activities can provide a cathartic publish and a way to connect with oneself on a deeper tier. It can be a form of self-expression and a means of reconnecting with one's inner child-like oddity. Many adults find comfort and delight in activities such as painting, writing, or playing a musical instrument. These activities can serve as a form of therapy, allowing individual to procedure and operate through their emotions in a safe and constructive way. Engaging in artistic activities can also help adults develop important skills such as forbearance, tenacity, and care to particular. These skills can be transferred to other area of lifetime, such as problem-solving at operate or maintaining healthy relationship. Creativity and artistic development can have a profound effect on one's overall well-being and mental wellness. Engaging in creative activities can reduce strain, anxiousness, and slump, as it provides a vent for self-expression and helps individual focusing on the present minute. Study have shown that creative activities such as painting, writing, or playing a musical instrument can increase positive emotions and improve overall climate. Art therapy has been used as a therapeutic instrument to help individual cope with injury, sorrow, and other emotional challenge. By engaging in artistic activities, individual can tap into their inner creativity and discover new way of understanding themselves and the world around them. This can lead to a greater sense of self-awareness and personal growth. Encouraging creativity and the development of artistic skills at all age is important for both children and adults. For young children, engaging in artistic activities allows them to explore their creativity and develop important social and emotional skills. For adults, artistic activities provide a means of self-expression, holistic heal, and personal growth. Irrespective of years, fostering creativity and artistic development can have numerous benefits, including improved problem-solving skills, enhanced emotional well-being, and a deeper link to oneself and others. By promoting creativity and artistic development at all age, we can create a more vibrant and fulfilled fellowship.

IX. SENIOR YEARS

In the senior years of life, there is often a shifting in focusing and priority. Many individuals in this phase are retired or nearing retreat, and thus have more time to dedicate to personal pursuit, including the development of artistic skills and the chase of creativeness. This point of life can be a golden opportunity for seniors to fully immerse themselves in the arts and explore their creative potential. Retreat offers a newfound exemption, allowing seniors to engage in activities they may not have had the time for during their working years. Whether it be painting, sculpt, writing, or music, the senior years can be a time of self-expression and artistic increase. One of the key advantage of pursuing artistic development in the senior years is the wealth of life experience that older individuals bring to their creative endeavor. Through years of live, seniors have accumulated a comprehensiveness of knowledge and soundness that can be channeled into their artistic Creation. This deepness of experience can bring a unique view and deepness to their art, as they draw upon a life of memory, emotion, and observation. This rich tapes of life can serve as a fountainhead of aspiration, fueling the innovation of fundamental and thought-provoking work of art. Engaging in artistic pursuit in the senior years offers a throng of cognitive and emotional benefits. Inquiry has shown that participating in creative activities can help improve cognitive operate, remembering, and overall mental well-being. The process of creating art involves critical think, problem-solving, and to utilize of multiple sense, stimulating the psyche and promoting neural connection. Artistic manifestation has been found to reduce strain, relieve symptom of slump and anxiousness, and enhance overall emotional well-being. For seniors, who may be grappling with the challenge of aging, the arts can provide a therapeutic vent and a sense of aim and fulfillment. The senior years offer a unique opportunity for intergenerational learn and collaboration. Many community and organization offer workshop and program that bring together individuals of different age group to engage in creative pursuit. This intergenerational interchange can be incredibly enriching, as older individuals have the opportunity to deal their knowledge and skills with younger generation, while also learning from and being inspired by their youthful counterpart. This collaborative surroundings foster a sense of community and link, bridging the coevals break and creating bond through a shared love for the arts. It is important to recognize that artistic development in the senior years is not limited to those who have had previous experience or formal preparation in the arts. In fact, for many seniors, the senior years may mark the first time they have the opportunity to fully explore their creative interest. The absence of any self-imposed expectation or squeeze to achieve can create a fertile soil for experiment and the development of a personal artistic flair. This exemption from opinion allows seniors to fully embrace the process of creating without any inhibition, leading to unexpected and delightful discovery. The senior years provide a unique and ideal time for individuals to pursue creativeness and develop artistic skills. With more time at their disposition, a wealth of life experience to draw upon, and an opportunity for intergenerational collaboration, seniors can fully immerse themselves in the arts and unleash their creative potential. The cognitive and emotional benefits of engaging in artistic activities can greatly enhance the overall well-being and caliber of life for seniors. Whether it is through painting, writing, music, or any other creative manifestation, the senior years can be a time of personal increase, self-discovery, and artistic fulfillment.

PROMOTING ACTIVE AGING THROUGH ARTISTIC ENGAGEMENT

Promoting active aging through artistic engagement is a powerful path to enhance the overall well-being and caliber of life in older adults. As individuals age, they may face various challenges, such as physical limitation, cognitive slump, and social isolation. Artistic engagement offers a throng of benefit that can help counteract these challenges and foster personal growth and fulfillment. Firstly, engaging in artistic activities promotes physical activity and improves overall physical wellness. Whether it is through dancing, paint, or playing a musical tool, older adults are able to engage in movement that stimulate their body and mind. This shape of physical activity not only improves muscularity potency and survival but also enhances tractability, coordination, and equilibrium, which are critical in maintaining overall physical wellness and preventing fall. Artistic engagement provides a means for creative and intellectual manifestation. Participating in artistic activities stimulates cognitive function, remembering, and problem-solving skill. Practicing a musical tool requires density and coordination, thus enhancing cognitive abilities and encouraging mental nimbleness. Artistic engagement foster emotional well-being and psychological resiliency. Through creative manifestation, individuals can explore and convey their thinking, feeling, and emotion, which can be particularly beneficial for older adults who may face various emotional challenges associated with aging, such as sorrow, aloneness, or a sense of aimlessness. Artistic engagement can serve as an instrument for self-reflection and self-expression, allowing individuals to gain a deeper understand of themselves and find a positive vent for their emotion. Artistic engagement can combat social isolation and foster social link. Participating in art class, workshop, or grouping performance promotes social interaction and provides opportunity for older adults to connect with like-minded individuals, deal experiences, and develop meaningful relationship. This social engagement is crucial for mental well-being and can alleviate feeling of aloneness and isolation that older adults often experience. Engaging in artistic activities within a community setting can cultivate a sense of belong and aim, which are essential for leading a fulfilling life in older age. Promoting active aging through artistic engagement has the potential to challenge societal ageist attitude and promote an inclusive society. By focusing on the abilities and potential of older adults, rather than their limitation and stereotype, artistic engagement allows individuals to contribute to society and challenge preconceived notion about aging. Older adults have lived rich and diverse life, and engaging in artistic activities provides a boulevard for sharing their experiences, perspective, and soundness with younger generation. This intergenerational interchange foster mutual understand and regard, and helps build a society that values and includes individuals of all ages. Promoting active aging through artistic engagement offers numerous benefit for older adults, enhancing their physical, cognitive, emotional, and social well-being. This overture recognizes the potential for growth and developing at all stage of life and addresses the specific need and challenges faced by older adults. By embracing artistic engagement as a means to promote active aging, individuals can experience personal growth, develop new skill, and find fulfillment and delight in their later days. Promoting and supporting artistic engagement in older adults has the potential to create a more inclusive society that values individuals of all ages and challenges ageist narrative.

ARTISTIC ACTIVITIES IMPROVING COGNITIVE FUNCTION IN SENIORS

Artistic activities have been found to have a positive effect on cognitive function in seniors. As individuals age, the brain naturally undergoes change, which can result in cognitive decline and a decrease in overall brain function. Engaging in artistic activities such as paint, drawing, or euphony can help counteract these effect and improve cognitive abilities. One path in which artistic activities improve cognitive function in seniors is through the arousal of the brain. When seniors engage in artistic endeavors, they are required to use various cognitive skills, such as problem-solving, memory remember, and spatial reason. These activities challenge the brain and coerce it to work, which can help improve cognitive function. Painting or drawing requires to utilize of hand-eye coordination and fine centrifugal skills, which can enhance overall cognitive abilities. Euphony activities, such as learning to play a tool or sing, stimulate different areas of the brain and heighten memory, attention, and words skills. Artistic activities also have the possible to improve cognitive function by promoting neuroplasticity. Neuroplasticity refer to the brain's power to change and reorganize itself in reaction to new experience or learn. When seniors engage in artistic activities, they are exposing their brain to new and stimulating experience, which can promote the establishment of new neural connection and strengthen existing one. This, in turning, can lead to improved cognitive function and better overall brain health. Study have shown that engagement in artistic activities can increase neural connectivity in areas of the brain associated with memory, attention, and creativity, thus promoting neuroplasticity and cognitive betterment. Artistic activities can also provide seniors with a sense of purpose and fulfillment, which can have significant positive effect on their cognitive function. As individuals age, they may experience a departure of individuality or a decrease in meaningful activities, which can contribute to cognitive decline. Engaging in artistic endeavors allows seniors to express their creativity, build new skills, and find purpose, leading to improved cognitive function. Artistic activities can also provide a sense of social link and engagement, which has been linked to cognitive health. When seniors participate in art class or join art community, they have the chance to interact with others who deal similar interest, leading to increased socializing and cognitive arousal. Artistic activities have been found to improve cognitive function in seniors through various mechanism. By stimulating the brain, promoting neuroplasticity, and providing a sense of purpose, engagement in artistic endeavors can lead to enhanced cognitive abilities in the elderly. As the senior universe continues to grow, it is crucial to promote and encourage artistic activities as a mean to improve cognitive health and overall well-being. It is important to increase consciousness and supporting for program that promote creativity and the developing of artistic skills in individuals of all age, including seniors. By doing so, we can help seniors maintain and even improve their cognitive function, leading to a higher caliber of lifetime in their golden days.

ARTISTIC PURSUITS ENHANCING OVERALL WELL-BEING AND QUALITY OF LIFE

Artistic pursuits, such as paint, write, and playing a tool, have been found to significantly enhance overall well-being and quality of life. Engaging in creative activities has been shown to uplift climate, reduce stress levels, and improve overall mental health. Inquiry has consistently suggested that participating in artistic endeavors leads to increased levels of happiness and life gratification. This can be attributed to the fact that the creative procedure allows individuals to express themselves freely, fostering a sense of self-discovery and personal growth. Artistic pursuits provide individuals with a means of loosening and escape, enabling them to detach from the struggle and pressures of daily life. Through the act of creation, individuals immerse themselves in a state of flowing, where they become fully absorbed in the present minute and experience a sense of eternity. This power to immerse oneself in the creative procedure has been likened to a shape of speculation, as it allows individuals to attain a state of mindfulness and attain a deeper understanding of themselves. In plus to improving mental well-being, engaging in artistic pursuits has also been linked to various physical health benefits. Study have found that participating in activities such as drawing or painting can help reduce blood pressure and lower marrow pace, which in turning, reduces the danger of cardiovascular disease. Involving oneself in artistic endeavors has been shown to enhance cognitive abilities. The act of creation requires individuals to think outside the corner, come up with innovative solution, and make connection between seemingly unrelated idea. These mental process help improve cognitive tractability, problem-solving skill, and critical think abilities. It can be argued that artistic pursuits serve as an exercising for the psyche, providing it with the arousal necessary for growth and developing. Artistic pursuits have also been found to enhance social connectedness, thereby improving one's overall quality of life. Engaging in creative activities provides individuals with a program to connect with others who deal similar interest. This fosters a sense of belonging and community, which is vital for mental and emotional well-being. Whether it be joining a community painting grade or participating in a local dramaturgy output, engaging in artistic pursuits allows individuals to interact and collaborate with like-minded individuals. This not only promotes social participation but also provides a boulevard for personal growth and self-discovery. Artistic pursuits have the potential to create cultural awareness and understanding. By engaging in creative activities, individuals are exposed to different perspectives, culture, and tradition. This vulnerability fosters empathy and pity, as it allows individuals to see the globe through the sense of others. Consequently, artistic pursuits can help break down barrier and promote social concord. Engaging in artistic endeavors can provide a means of self-expression for marginalized group in society. Through art, individuals who may feel disenfranchised or overlooked can shed illumination on their experience and contribute to the larger narrative. This promotes inclusivity and variety, fostering a society that value and celebrates the magnificence of different perspectives. Engaging in artistic pursuits has been found to significantly enhance overall well-being and quality of life. Through the act of creation, individuals experience increased levels of happiness, reduced stress levels, and improved mental health. Artistic endeavors provide individuals with a means of loosening, allowing them to detach from the pressures of daily life and immerse themselves in a state of flowing. Engaging in artistic pursuits has been linked to various physical health benefits, such as reduced blood pressure and enhanced cognitive abilities. Artistic pursuits foster social connectedness, providing individuals with a sense of belonging and community. Artistic pursuits have the force to create cultural awareness and understanding, allowing individuals to engage with different perspectives and contribute to a more inclusive society. Thus, it can be argued that encouraging creativeness and the developing of artistic skill at all age is essential for achieving overall well-being and a higher quality of life.

ENCOURAGING INTERGENERATIONAL ARTISTIC COLLABORATIONS

In plus to fostering creativeness and artistic skills at all ages, it is essential to promote intergenerational artistic collaborations. By bringing together individual from different age group, valuable exchanges of knowledge, experiences, and perspective can occur, ultimately enriching the creative process. Intergenerational collaborations have the potential to transcend both generational and artistic boundary, allowing for unique and innovative Creation. One of the key advantage of encouraging intergenerational artistic collaborations is the opportunity for knowledge transfer between generations. Older individual, who have accumulated a rich of artistic experiences, can pass on their expertness to younger artists. These intergenerational exchanges allow for the conservation and diffusion of traditional artistic practice that might otherwise be lost. A seasoned carver can deal her sculpting techniques with a beginner carver, ensuring that the time-honored skills are not forgotten. This transmitting of knowledge foster a sense of persistence and can inspire younger artists to explore new possibility while grounding their work in the soundness of the preceding. Intergenerational collaborations promote a diverse array of perspective and idea. Each generation brings its unique social, cultural, and historical backdrop, shaping their artistic sensibility. By collaborating across generations, artists have the opportunity to challenge their own assumption and explore unfamiliar perspective. This heightened exposure to diverse viewpoint can lead to the creation of artwork that challenges societal norm, break down stereotype, and foster greater understanding between generations. A collaboration between a young graffito artist and an older muralist might lead to a powerful unification of street art and traditional techniques, creating a visually stunning mural that explores contemporary social issue. Intergenerational collaborations also have the potential to stimulate creativeness by encouraging artists to think beyond their usual artistic routine. When artists from different generations come together, they have the opportunity to experiment with unfamiliar artistic medium or approach. This exposure to new techniques can invigorate their creative process, giving rising to innovative and unconventional work. An older cat amount, accustomed to working with oil, might collaborate with a young digital artist, leading to the creation of mixed-media artwork that combines traditional painting techniques with cutting-edge digital use. These collaborations challenge artists to step outside their solace zone and push the boundary of their artistic exercise. Intergenerational collaborations foster a sense of community and link between artists of different ages. Creative endeavor often requires working in isolation, which can be isolating and limiting for artists. By bringing individual together across generations, collaborations provide opportunity for artists to connect with their peer and find supporting from experienced mentor. This sense of community can be particularly beneficial for young artists who may lack direction and resource. Through collaborations, they can find direction, supporting, and aspiration that can propel their artistic developing. These collaborations can combat ageism by promoting mutual regard and admiration for artists of all ages. Breaking down this barrier can encourage dialog and understand, leading to a more inclusive and supportive artistic community. Encouraging intergenerational artistic collaborations is crucial for the developing of artistic skills and the nurture of creativeness in individual of all ages. Through knowledge transfer, diverse perspective, creative arousal, and community construction, artists can benefit greatly from collaborating across generations. By fostering these intergenerational exchanges, we can create a vivacious and inclusive artistic community that transcends generational boundary and produces innovative and impactful work of art.

BRIDGING GENERATIONAL GAPS THROUGH SHARED ARTISTIC EXPERIENCES

One of the most powerful ways to bridge generational gaps is through shared artistic experiences. Art has the ability to transcend age and bring people together, fostering a feel of unity and understanding among individuals of different generations. As we age, our perspectives and experiences evolve, making it sometimes challenging to connect with those from different age group. Art can serve as a common soil that allows people to connect, convey, and appreciate one another's unique perspectives. Through shared artistic experiences, individuals of different generations can gain a deeper understanding of one another, breaking down stereotypes and fostering meaningful connection. Artistic experiences have the force to provide a valuable program for intergenerational dialogue. When people engage in artistic activity together, they have the opportunity to express themselves creatively and communicate their thinking and feeling in a nonverbal and nonthreatening way. This can be especially beneficial in bridging generational gaps, as older adults may have trouble relating to younger individuals due to divergence in lifetime experiences and value. When individuals come together in a creative set, they are able to connect on a profound level, transcending age and opening the doorway to meaningful dialogue. Through art, individuals of all age can share their perspectives, learn from one another, and gain a deeper understanding of the surrounding globe. Shared artistic experiences can help dispel stereotypes and break down barrier between generations. In fellowship, there are often stereotypes associated with different age group, perpetuating assumption that lead to misunderstanding and division. When individuals come together through art, these stereotypes can be challenged and dismantled. Art allows individuals to express themselves freely, providing an infinite where people can showcase their unique talent and perspectives regardless of age. By creating and appreciating art together, people can see beyond age as a define element and instead focus on the creativeness and endowment that each individual possess. Shared artistic experiences can inspire and foster creativeness across generations. When people of different age come together to create art, they have the opportunity to learn from one another and explore new perspectives. Younger individuals can learn from the experiences and soundness of older generations, while older adults can be inspired by the fresh idea and innovative think of the younger generation. This cross-pollination of creativeness can lead to the developing of unique artistic expression and push boundary of artistic possibility. By sharing and collaborating in artistic endeavor, individuals of different generations can inspire one another, leading to personal and artistic growth for all involved. Bridging generational gaps through shared artistic experiences is a powerful instrument for fostering unity, understanding, and creativeness among individuals of different age. Art has the ability to transcend age and open door to meaningful dialogue, dispelling stereotypes, and inspiring personal and artistic growth. By engaging in shared artistic activity, individuals of different generations can connect on a profound level, gain a deeper understanding of one another, and appreciate each other's unique perspectives. It is through these shared experiences that generational gaps can be bridged, bringing people together and creating a more inclusive fellowship.

SENIORS AS MENTORS AND ROLE MODELS FOR YOUNGER GENERATIONS

Another path to encourage creativity and the development of artistic skills at all ages is to utilize the expertness and experience of seniors as mentors and role models for younger generations. Seniors have a wealth of knowledge and experience that they can pass on to the younger generation, and by doing so, they not only help to foster creativity and artistic development but also bridge the generation gap and create a sense of community. Seniors can serve as mentors by sharing their skills and knowledge with younger individuals who are interested in pursuing artistic endeavor. An elderly cat amount can provide direction and advice to a young aspiring artist on technique, makeup, and coloration hypothesis. The exchange of knowledge between generations not only enhances the artistic skills of the younger individual but also allows the senior to pass on their days of soundness and experience. This mentorship kinship benefit both party, as the senior has a sense of aim and fulfillment by passing on their knowledge, and the younger individual gain valuable insight and direction in their artistic journey. In plus to serving as mentors, seniors can also act as role models for younger generations. Many seniors have dedicated their life to pursuing their artistic passion, and by showcasing their work and achievement, they inspire and motivate younger individuals to follow their own creative pursuit. Seniors can exhibit their art in local gallery or participate in community art show, providing an opportunity for younger individuals to view their work and learn from their artistic journey. By highlighting the accomplishments of seniors in the arts, younger generations can see that creativity and artistic development are lifelong pursuit that can continue to bring delight and fulfillment well into old age. The mien of seniors as mentors and role models also helps to bridge the generation gap and create a sense of community. In now's fast-paced and technology-driven globe, there can be a disconnection between generations, with little opportunity for meaningful interaction and exchange of idea. By involving seniors in mentor and role model activity, younger individuals have the opportunity to build relationship and learn from individuals who have different lifetime experience and perspective. This intergenerational exchange foster understanding, empathy, and admiration for the various background and talents that exist within a community. Seniors can also benefit from this interaction by feeling valued and respected for their knowledge and contributions, leading to a greater sense of belong and connection. Involving seniors as mentors and role models in the artistic development of younger generations helps to break down stereotype and challenge ageism. By showcasing the talents and accomplishments of seniors in the arts, society can shift its percent of aging and recognize that creativity and artistic expression are not limited to specific age group. This promotes a more inclusive and age-friendly society where individuals of all ages are encouraged to pursue their artistic passion and lend to the cultural cloth of their community. Seniors can play a crucial role in encouraging creativity and the development of artistic skills at all ages. By serving as mentors and role models, seniors can deal their knowledge and expertness, invigorate younger individuals, bridge the generation gap, and challenge ageism. It is important to recognize and harness the talents and contributions of seniors in the arts, as they have a wealth of knowledge and experience that can greatly enrich the artistic development of younger generations. By promoting intergenerational collaboration and understanding, society can create an surrounding that nurtures creativity and artistic expression for individuals of all ages. The grandness of creativity and the development of artistic skills cannot be understated. It is well known that engaging in creative activities and exercising artistic talent has numerous benefit at all ages. From the early stage of puerility to maturity and beyond, creativity plays a significant role in enhancing cognitive abilities, emotional well-being, and personal growth. It is essential that individuals are encouraged to be creative and foster their artistic development from a young age. First and foremost, creativity is integral to cognitive development in children. Engaging in creative activities such as draw, paint, or playing a musical tool stimulates the psyche and helps build neural connection. Inquiry has shown that children who are exposed to art and encouraged to be creative lean to have better problem-solving skills and higher IQ. They become more adaptable and flexible thinker, as they are able to approach challenge from different angle and find innovative solution. Creativity boost remembering and improves care bridge, which are valuable skills for academic achiever. It is crucial that parent, teachers, and caregiver provide children with ample opportunities to engage in creative activities and explore their artistic abilities. Creativity also plays a key role in emotional well-being. Masses of all ages face strain, anxiousness, and other negative emotion, and engaging in creative endeavors can serve as a powerful vent for this emotion. Expressing oneself through art allows individuals to release pent-up feeling and find comfort. Artistic activities, such as paint or write, can serve as a shape of therapy and help individuals process their emotion and experience. Creativity fosters self-expression and self-confidence. When individuals engage in creative activities, they feel a sense of achievement and congratulate in their operate, which boosts their self-esteem. This, in turning, contributes to their overall emotional well-being and helps them navigate through lifetime's challenge more effectively. Fostering creativity and artistic skills has a positive effect on personal growth. Creativity encourages individuals to think outside the corner, take risk, and embrace new idea. It promotes a sense of oddity and a want to explore the globe and learn new thing. Engaging in creative activities fosters a sense of individuality and individualism. When individuals are encouraged to express themselves artistically, they develop a unique flair and vocalization that reflects their personality. This leads to the uncovering of individual strength and passion that can shape personal and professional pursuit. Creativity fosters collaboration and teamwork. When individuals engage in creative activities together, they learn to communicate effectively, respect one another's idea, and operate towards a common finish. These interpersonal skills are invaluable in all aspect of lifetime, whether it be in the work or in personal relationship. Creativity and the development of artistic skills are crucial for individuals of all ages. Engaging in creative activities enhances cognitive abilities, promotes emotional well-being, and contributes to personal growth. It is essential that creativity is encouraged and artistic development is fostered from a young age. Parent, teachers, and caregiver should provide children with opportunities to engage in creative endeavors and explore their artistic abilities. Individuals should continue to cultivate creativity throughout their lives, as it has numerous benefit for personal and professional development. By prioritizing creativity and artistic development, individuals can unlock their full possible, enrich their lives, and make valuable contribution to fellowship.

X. CONCLUSION

Creativity is a fundamental facet of human developing that should be nurtured and encouraged at all ages. Through creative activity and experience, individual are able to express themselves, explore their imagination, and develop important artistic skill. By providing opportunity for creativity to flourish, we can foster personal increase, enhance cognitive ability, and lend to a more vibrant and innovative society. It is essential for educator, parent, and community to prioritize the integrating of artistic and creative experience into curriculum and daily routine. Fostering a supportive and inclusive surroundings that value and celebrate creativity is crucial in promoting artistic developing. Recognizing and valuing creativity as an important effort for masses of all ages can lead to a more expressive, diverse, and culturally enriched society. It is imperative that we continue to prioritize and champ creativity as a vital element of individual and societal increase.

RECAP OF THE IMPORTANCE OF ENCOURAGING CREATIVITY AND ARTISTIC DEVELOPMENT AT ALL AGES

It is evident that encouraging creativity and artistic development at all ages is of utmost grandness. Creativity is not limited to a specific age grouping ; it is a fundamental facet of human nature that should be nurtured throughout a person's life. By encouraging creativity, individuals are able to develop skill that can benefit them in various aspects of their life. Artistic development plays a crucial part in promoting self-expression and improving mental well-being. It allows individuals to explore their emotion, thinking, and experience through different artistic medium. Artistic development can enhance cognitive ability, such as critical think, problem-solving, and decision-making. By engaging in creative activities, individuals are challenged to think outside the corner and find innovative solution to problem. Encouraging creativity and artistic development at all ages foster personal growth and self-discovery. It allows individuals to discover their unique talent, strength, and passion, and encourages them to pursue their artistic endeavor. Engaging in creative activities can provide individuals with a sense of purpose and fulfillment. It allows them to express themselves authentically and contribute to society in meaningful way. Encouraging creativity and artistic development at all ages has numerous societal benefit. It fosters a culture of invention and intellectual growth, driving progression and advancement in various fields. It also promotes cultural understanding and admiration. Through art, individuals are able to communicate across different language, culture, and background. Artistic expression has the power to challenge stereotype, encourage dialog, and promote empathy and regard for diverse perspective. Encouraging creativity and artistic development at all ages can have positive effect on mental wellness. Engaging in creative activities can provide individuals with a sense of purpose and belong, reducing feeling of aloneness and isolation. It can also serve as a shape of therapy, allowing individuals to procedure and mend from emotional injury. Artistic expression has been shown to reduce strain, anxiousness, and slump, promoting overall well-being. It is essential to recognize and valuate the grandness of encouraging creativity and artistic development at all ages. By doing so, individuals are provided with opportunity for self-expression, personal growth, and intellectual arousal. Fellowship as a whole benefit from a culture that values creativity, as it promotes invention, cultural understanding, and enhanced mental well-being. It is crucial that educational institution, community, and individuals alike prioritize and supporting effort to foster creativity and artistic development at all stage of lifetime. Through this effort, the true possible of individuals and fellowship can be achieved, leading to a more vibrant, inclusive, and prosperous globe.

RESTATEMENT OF THESIS STATEMENT

Creativeness is an essential facet of human developing, and it is crucial to encourage and nurture artistic skills at all stage of lifetime. From early puerility to late maturity, individuals possess a unique capability to think creatively and express themselves through various art form. By fostering creativeness, individuals can unlock their potential, enhance cognitive ability, and develop a deeper understand of themselves and the surrounding globe. Engaging in artistic activity promotes emotional well-being and serves as a vent for self-expression. It is imperative to encourage creativeness and the developing of artistic skills across all age group, as it contributes to personal increase, social interaction, and cultural enrichment.

CALL TO ACTION: SOCIETY MUST PRIORITIZE AND SUPPORT ARTISTIC GROWTH AND CREATIVITY AT ALL STAGES OF LIFE

It is crucial for fellowship to prioritize and support artistic growth and creativity at every phase of lifetime. As seen throughout this test, creativity and artistic development have numerous benefit for individuals of all ages. Whether it is through cognitive development, emotional manifestation, or overall well-being, engaging in artistic activity has been proven to enhance both physical and mental wellness. Promoting creativity from a young age can lead to increased problem-solving skill and adaptability, which are increasingly valuable in now's rapidly changing world. The obligation to nurture artistic growth does not solely lie with the individual, but also with the community and fellowship at large. It is imperative for schools, parent, and policymakers to provide the necessary resource and opportunity for individuals to explore their artistic talent and passion. This can range from implementing comprehensive arts teaching program in schools, fostering collaboration between artist and community, or establishing financing and support for aspiring artist. It is crucial to break down the barrier and stigma associated with pursuing a vocation in the arts, and to cultivate an surrounding that value and supporting individuals in their artistic endeavor. By doing so, fellowship can tap into the immense possible that lies within every individual, fostering a civilization of creativity, invention, and personal growth. Only by recognizing and prioritizing artistic growth and creativity can we truly unlock the transformative force that lies within each of us. As the say goes, "Art enables us to find ourselves and lose ourselves at the same clock.". Let us embrace and champion the arts, for they hold the fundamental to a bright, more harmonious, and imaginative world. Let us cultivate creativity and artistic development at all ages, and together, let us paint a masterpiece of a fellowship.

BIBLIOGRAPHY

Phyllis Gelineau. 'Integrating the Arts Across the Elementary School Curriculum.' Cengage Learning, 1/1/2011

Robert Schirrmacher. 'Art and Creative Development for Young Children.' J. Englebright Fox, Cengage Learning, 1/1/2011

Roberta Michnick Golinkoff. 'Play Learning.' How Play Motivates and Enhances Children's Cognitive and Social-Emotional Growth, Dorothy Singer, Oxford University Press, 8/24/2006

Elizabeth M. Allegretti. 'Improving Kindergarten Students' Fine Motor Skills Through Art-based Occupational Therapy Interventions.' Central Connecticut State University, 1/1/2000

Institute of Medicine. 'From Neurons to Neighborhoods.' The Science of Early Childhood Development, National Research Council, National Academies Press, 11/13/2000

Jean Van't Hul. 'The Artful Parent.' Simple Ways to Fill Your Family's Life with Art and Creativity, Shambhala Publications, 6/11/2019

Ann Pelo. 'Rethinking Early Childhood Education.' Rethinking Schools, 1/1/2008

Mindy R. Carter. 'Art as an Agent for Social Change.' Hala Mreiwed, BRILL, 10/12/2020

Elif M. Gokcigdem. 'Fostering Empathy Through Museums.' Rowman & Littlefield, 7/19/2016

Robert Gibson. 'Bridge the Culture Gaps.' A toolkit for effective collaboration in the diverse, global workplace, Quercus, 3/8/2022

Ernst Wagner. 'Arts and Cultural Education in a World of Diversity.' ENO Yearbook 1, Lígia Ferro, Springer, 4/2/2019

Jacob Morgan. 'The Employee Experience Advantage.' How to Win the War for Talent by Giving Employees the Workspaces they Want, the Tools they Need, and a Culture They Can Celebrate, John Wiley & Sons, 3/1/2017

Olivier Bouin. 'A Manifesto for Social Progress.' Ideas for a Better Society, Marc Fleurbaey, Cambridge University Press, 8/30/2018

Minghai Zheng. 'The Power of Innovation.' Harnessing the Creative Potential of Individuals and Organizations, Amazon Digital Services LLC - Kdp, 8/13/2023

Betsy McKenna. 'Art Workshop for Children.' How to Foster Original Thinking with more than 25 Process Art Experiences, Barbara Rucci, Quarry Books, 11/1/2016

Duffy, Bernadette. 'Supporting Creativity And Imagination In The Early Years.' McGraw-Hill Education (UK), 5/1/2006

Bruce Robertson. 'The Teaching Delusion 2: Teaching Strikes Back.' Hodder Education, 9/24/2021

Carl Patterson. 'Critical Thinking And Problem Solving.' Advanced Strategies and Reasoning Skills to Increase Your Decision Making. A Systematic Approach to Master Logic, Avoid Mistakes and Be a Creative Problem Solver, Independently Published, 1/4/2020

Grégoire Borst. 'The Cambridge Handbook of Cognitive Development.' Olivier Houdé, Cambridge University Press, 3/3/2022

Ruchi Dwivedi, Tulika Saxena. 'Business Management and Entrepreneurship.' Ashutosh Priya, OrangeBooks Publication, 7/26/2023

Brian Roet. 'The Confidence To Be Yourself.' How to boost your self-esteem, Little, Brown Book Group, 5/15/2014

Brian K. Hemphill. 'The Elements of Creative and Expressive Artistry.' A Philosophy for Creating Everything Artistic, iUniverse, 9/6/2011

Bonnie Thomas. 'Creative Expression Activities for Teens.' Exploring Identity through Art, Craft and Journaling, Jessica Kingsley Publishers, 6/15/2011

Betty Lelly. 'Spiritual Self Discovery and Self Expression.' Charles Lelly, AuthorHouse, 11/25/2002

Steve Pavlina. 'Personal Development for Smart People.' ReadHowYouWant.com, 7/1/2010

Institute of Medicine. 'Transforming the Workforce for Children Birth Through Age 8.' A Unifying Foundation, National Research Council, National Academies Press, 7/23/2015

Nan E. Hathaway. 'The Learner-Directed Classroom.' Developing Creative Thinking Skills Through Art, Diane B. Jaquith, Teachers College Press, 4/26/2015

Susan E. Jackson. 'The Creative Visual Arts Experience.' A Phenomenology of Artistic Adolescents and Their Teachers, University of Houston, 1/1/2010